Leckie×Leckie

HIGHER
Business Management

er

Anne Bradley ✕ Derek McInally

ISBN 978-1-84372-710-1

Published by
Leckie & Leckie Ltd, 4 Queen Street, Edinburgh, EH2 1JE
Tel: 0131 220 6831 Fax: 0131 225 9987
enquiries@leckieandleckie.co.uk   www.leckieandleckie.co.uk

Special thanks to
documen (design and page makeup),
Jill A. Laidlaw (copy-editing),
Caleb Rutherford (cover-design),
Jennifer Shaw (proofreading).

A CIP Catalogue record for this book is available from the British Library.

Leckie & Leckie makes every effort to ensure that all paper used in our
books is made from wood pulp obtained from well-managed forests,
controlled sources and recycled wood or fibre.

® Leckie & Leckie is a registered trademark

Leckie & Leckie Ltd is a division of Huveaux plc.

Acknowledgements

We would like to thank the following for permission to reproduce their material:

SQA for permission to reproduce quotes and past examination case studies.

The Scotsman Publications Ltd for the article
'Sweet Taste of Turnaround Success'.

Simple Shoes (AMG Footwear)

Every effort has been made to trace the copyright holders and to obtain
their permission for the use of copyright material. Leckie & Leckie will
gladly receive information enabling them to rectify any error or omission
in subsequent editions.

CONTENTS

Introduction

What will I learn from this book?

How will this book help me?

The coursework and the examination

What's in this book?

How should I use this book?

WHAT WILL I LEARN FROM THIS BOOK?

You will learn about the skills you need to achieve the best possible grade in Higher Business Management. You will learn how to answer the type of questions you will be asked in the examination and unit assessments. There are worked examples of answers, as well as tips that will show you how to boost your grade.

HOW WILL THIS BOOK HELP ME?

This book will take you stage by stage through the skills you need for your Business Management course. There are practice unit assessments (often referred to as 'NABs'), which will prepare you for your end of unit assessment. This book will give you advice and answer many of the questions you have about how to do well in Higher Business Management.

THE COURSEWORK AND THE EXAMINATION

The Higher Business Management coursework involves three internal assessments called unit assessments. These units can be taken at the end of studying the units or at the end of the course. They are 'closed book' assessments which means that you cannot rely on notes or any other study aids during the test.

There are basically two units in Higher Business Management: *Business Enterprise* and *Business Decision Areas*. Business Decision Areas is a double unit so it is perhaps easier to see this as two areas of study. An end of unit assessment will test your knowledge of each area. The assessment cannot possibly cover every aspect of the course and so the end of unit assessments 'sample' tests only some of the topic. However there is no way of telling which areas will be tested and you should use the end of unit assessments to prepare for the final examination by studying the whole unit in detail.

Each of the unit assessments comprise of a case study followed by a number of questions totalling 40 marks. You have an hour to complete each assessment.

The following tables set out the unit assessment requirements for Higher Business Management.

Unit Assessment

Unit 1	Areas of Study	Internal Assessment
Business Enterprise	Business in Contemporary Society Business Information and IT Decision Making in Business	Marked out of 40 Pass mark 50%

Unit 1 also includes the study of **Internal Organisations** which is not assessed in the end of unit assessment.

While Internal Organisations is not assessed in the end of unit assessment, it will be assessed in the final examination.

Unit 2	Areas of Study	Internal Assessment
Business Decision Areas: Marketing and Operations	Marketing Operations	Marked out of 40 Pass mark 50% Assessment samples both areas
Business Decision Areas: Finance and Human Resource Management	Finance Human Resource Management	Marked out of 40 Pass mark 50% Assessment samples both areas

 See Chapter 2 for more information on internal assessment.

The Final Examination

You will have to sit one paper at the end of the course during the SQA diet.

The paper lasts for 2 hours 30 minutes and it is marked out of 100.

In general:

- 50-59% will give you a grade **C** award;
- 60-69% a grade **B** award, and
- 70+% a grade **A** award.

Paper	Content	Marks
Section One	Involves a 750-word case study from which you will identify some management problems. There are normally between seven and eight questions. All questions are compulsory in this section.	50 marks
Section Two	Two questions from five should be attempted.	25 marks each question or a total of 50 marks

 See Chapter 3 for more information about the final exam.

WHAT'S IN THIS BOOK?

Chapter 1

This chapter provides you with a knowledge of the basic skills in answering questions which includes the use of the 'command' words. This section will increase your awareness of what is being asked and how to go about answering questions to boost your chances of gaining full marks.

Chapter 1 will focus on the actual wording of questions which will prepare you for the internal assessment and the final examination.

Chapter 2

This chapter looks at the internal unit assessments, also known as NABs. You must pass the internal assessments if you are to be awarded an overall grade in Higher Business Management.

This chapter will prepare you with practical examples which cover the areas of assessment. Use this chapter for the end of unit assessments but also in preparation for the external examination since the questions are similar to those you will find in the SQA diet.

Chapter 3

Here we look at the final examination. This will bring together all the tips you have learnt throughout the book to boost your overall score in the final exam. This chapter will focus on technique. There are examples of questions from past papers showing good and bad practice from candidates' work. Use this section to realise the standard that is expected of you in the final exam.

HOW SHOULD I USE THIS BOOK?

This book can help you at various points in your course. Dip into it when you need to. But make sure you come back and study it more thoroughly when you prepare for end of unit assessments, prelims and the final exam.

That's when you will find that the advice, tips and skills in this book will boost your grade.

1 Command Words

COMMAND WORDS

 From SQA External Assessment Report

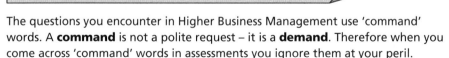

'Candidates who know how to handle the list of command words generally perform better.'

The questions you encounter in Higher Business Management use 'command' words. A **command** is not a polite request – it is a **demand**. Therefore when you come across 'command' words in assessments you ignore them at your peril.

Frequently a question might contain more than one command word so be careful that you are answering the full question and not simply one part of it.

 Underline or highlight the command word(s) used in questions to ensure that you focus on how you are expected to answer. Take care to make sure that your response to a question relates to what is ACTUALLY asked.

Below is a list of the command words which have been used in end of unit assessments and recent past papers. Learn their meaning. Use this page whenever you are answering a question until you are familiar with the meaning of each command.

Command Word	Definition
Compare	Point out similarities and differences between two or more factors. You might also be asked to state a preference. You should try to emphasise or stress the unique features of each in comparison to the other(s).
Example	**Compare** the relative costs and benefits of primary and secondary information.
Distinguish	Identify the differences between two or more factors i.e. what makes them different or separate from each other.
Example	**Distinguish** between a centralised and a decentralised structure.
Describe	Provide a detailed description. One word answers for 'descriptions' are never acceptable, you must use a sentence(s). While examples are not usually credited in Higher Business Management you may find they help you in a description.
Example	**Describe** the benefits of using the internet to market products.
Discuss	Examine closely taking account of strengths and weaknesses in an argument; for and against. This cannot simply be a list – points must be developed. Although negatives and positives should be explored, it is not necessary in all cases. It is important that you carefully read and fully understand the question being asked.
Example	**Discuss** the role of appraisal and its ability to motivate staff.

Explain	Give a detailed explanation of the impact of some course of action. Give reasons for your points – again remember that sometimes giving examples can help the examiner understand what you are writing about.
Example	**Explain** the reasons why a competitor might wish to take over a firm that is not making a great deal of profit.
Identify/name	State or list. This calls for brief points. In a question this instruction will often be used along with another more demanding command word, e.g. **justify** (*see below*).
Example	**Identify** a source of assistance that may be available to an exporter.
Justify	Give good reasons to support suggestions or explain the reason(s) for your suggestion. This can be a simple statement of why something has been chosen or suggested.
Example	**Identify** and **justify** three alternative sources of long-term finance which could be used by a firm taking over a rival.
Outline	State the main features. This calls for a number of different points but not in great detail.
Example	**Outline** the reasons for preparing budgets.
Finally, **describe, discuss** and **explain** can all be used with	
Advantage and disadvantage	Pros and cons of something – at least one **advantage** and one **disadvantage** should be given to get the full mark allocation. However you need to take care that you do not just give a straight negative of an advantage as a disadvantage – this will not gain any marks. Points must be **described, discussed** or **explained**.
Example	**Describe** the **advantages** and **disadvantages** of branding to an organisation.

 Avoid bulleted lists with one or two words – it is too easy to miss out on enough detail to be awarded the full marks. Remember that the marks awarded to questions are an indication of the depth of answer being looked for by the examiner.

COMMAND WORDS IN ACTION

Look at the following examples of command words from recent past papers to help you to understand the importance and use of command words.

The first two examples deal with *external factors affecting the operation of business* from your study of Business in Contemporary Society.

> **Describe four external factors that can affect the success or failure of a business.** (4 marks)

Simply naming PESTEC factors will gain no marks at all.

This question is looking for four separate factors – described in full – in other words you need to **name** and **describe** four factors to get full marks. As you can see from the answer below, sometimes a quick example (e.g. mentioning e-commerce, flooding etc.) helps to make the description more complete.

 Government may introduce legislation that a business must abide by which can have costly implications. (1 mark) Most businesses also need to keep up-to-date with the latest technology for example using e-commerce to increase sales. (1 mark) An economic factor could be the number and strength of competitors in the same market, which can also affect the success of a business. (1 mark) Environmental factors, such as unexpected flooding or unseasonal weather, can also contribute to the failure of a business. (1 mark)

However ...

> **Identify and explain three economic factors that can affect the profitability of a business.** (6 marks)

This question is very specific. It allows you to gain 3 marks for the *simple naming of three factors* – but this is not enough to gain all 6 marks.

In order to gain the other 3 marks you need to give an explanation of the factors in relation to the profitability of a business. An example of a good answer to this question follows.

A recession (1 mark) can affect the profitability of a business as customers do not have the money to spend on an organisation's products and so profits shrink. (1 mark) Exchange rates (1 mark) can affect profitability because if UK sterling is high abroad then this may affect the possibility of doing business internationally. (1 mark) Inflation (1 mark) usually leads to increasing costs (e.g. raw materials or wages) and this may lead to less profits being made. (1 mark)

The next two examples deal with *the Role of the Entrepreneur* from your study of Business in Contemporary Society and *Entrepreneurial Structure* from your study of Internal Organisation.

Take care with this type of question. It is easy to think that role and structure are the same. They are not.

Describe the role of an entrepreneur in a business.

(4 marks)

Take care not to confuse an entrepreneur with a manager – you will gain no marks for the role of the manager.

This question simply requires you to write four detailed points about an entrepreneur in a business. The important thing to remember here is the question is asking you to **describe** the **role** of the entrepreneur – in other words what the entrepreneur actually does.

Here is a good answer to this question.

An entrepreneur is the person who combines the factors of production (land, labour and capital) to produce goods or services. (1 mark) The entrepreneur identifies future opportunities for the business by coming up with new ideas for making products. (1 mark) The entrepreneur is willing to take risks to allow the business to grow and become more efficient. (1 mark) The entrepreneur invests money in projects but is willing to lose money if the plan does not work out. (1 mark)

However...

> ## Explain the advantages and disadvantages of an entrepreneurial structure to an organisation. (4 marks)

This question is looking for a much more detailed understanding of the *advantages* and *disadvantages* of an *entrepreneurial structure*, NOT just a description of an entrepreneur.

The question wants you to show how the way an organisation is structured **affects** an organisation in a good way (**advantages**) and not such a good way (**disadvantages**). Note that the question uses the plural so as the mark allocation is 4 it is best to give two **advantages** and two **disadvantages** to gain the full allocation of the marks.

A good answer is given below.

An entrepreneurial structure is one where there are only one or two key decision makers. This can be an advantage when decisions have to be made quickly on a daily basis. (1 mark) There is also a greater chance that when decisions are made they are accurate, as the key decision makers usually have the most expertise. (1 mark) However disadvantages could be that the lack of consultation with other staff may be demotivating for them (1 mark) and also stress levels can be very high for the one or two staff responsible for making the decisions. (1 mark)

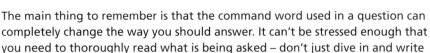

♪ See Chapter 3 for more information about the final exam.

The main thing to remember is that the command word used in a question can completely change the way you should answer. It can't be stressed enough that you need to thoroughly read what is being asked – don't just dive in and write what you 'think' is being asked just because you see some familiar words.

FOCUS ON THE COMMAND WORDS

More examples now to illustrate how the command word can affect how the question should be answered. This time it is exactly the same topic with the emphasis being on the command word used.

The first two examples are testing your knowledge of the decision making model – **type 1** simply requires that you write what you know about the benefits of using a decision making model to solve business problems, whereas **type 2** allows you to **name (identify)** the stages and also show that you understand why it is good to use this model. Remember **justify** usually means give a reason for following a certain course of action.

Question – type 1

> Describe the benefits of using a structured decision making model in order to solve a business problem.
>
> (5 marks)

A structured decision making model usually means that no rash decisions are made. (1 mark) The model allows the organisation to consider all the options and select the best. (1 mark) An organisation can identify its strengths and weaknesses and decide on the best way forward. (1 mark) Also if everybody knows what they are doing and why they are doing it they will be more motivated. (1 mark) Finally, using a structure ensures that any arrangements for resources can be put in place before the final solution is decided. (1 mark)

Question – type 2

> Identify stages of a structured decision making model and justify their use in solving business problems.
>
> (8 marks)

Gather information (1 mark) – this provides a business with a means of approaching problems so that no rash decisions are made. (1 mark) Analyse information (1 mark) – once sorted into a useful format the organisation can consider all the options and help decide what can or can't be done and what will help or hinder the progress made. (1 mark) One of the steps in the model includes communication to everyone involved (1 mark) because if everybody knows what they are doing and why they will be more motivated. (1 mark) The next stage is implementation. (1 mark) Using a structure ensures that any arrangements for resources can be put in place before implementing any solution. (1 mark)

The next two examples are testing your knowledge of branding – the first one needs you to show **what you know** whereas the second one needs you to show that you are **fully aware of the impact** of own branding to an organisation.

> When describing **disadvantages** it is a good idea to use an introductory word like **however** and then maybe using **also**. Remember 'discuss' usually means giving a balanced view of the **role** or **importance** of something you have studied. It is also a good idea when attempting a **'discuss'** question to start with a statement or definition of whatever it is you are going to **discuss** – it sets the scene and keeps you focussed.

Question – type 1

> ### Describe the advantages and disadvantages of branding to an organisation
> (4 marks)

A benefit of a well-known brand is instant recognition by the customer. (1 mark) This ensures that the customer will choose the brand before others and be loyal. (1 mark) However promotion costs can be high during the time needed to secure this amount of loyalty. (1 mark) Also, bad publicity for one product in a range can be very harmful to all products covered by the brand. (1 mark)

Question – type 2

> ### Discuss the advantages and disadvantages to an organisation such as Asda of selling own-brand products.
> (4 marks)

Asda has a range of goods made to its own specifications (*this is a good introduction which illustrates that you fully understand the concept of own brand*) which contains exactly what they want to put into it and which it then sells at a price of its own choosing. (1 mark) Selling own-brand products means that money can be saved on packaging and advertising. (1 mark) However own-brand products may be seen by some customers as being of lower quality than other brand names. (1 mark) Also, bad publicity for one product in a range can be very harmful to all products covered by the brand. (1 mark)

Can you see the difference?

2 Unit Assessment (NABs)

INTRODUCTION

 From SQA Internal Assessment Report

'The holistic nature of the NABs and their length make them similar to the final exam. The internal assessment process provides a good opportunity to familiarise candidates with the list of command words and their different meanings.

This is excellent preparation for the final exam.'

Part of your course involves internal assessment. This is where you will do an end of Unit Assessment in examination conditions. These assessments are *'closed book'* meaning you cannot refer to any notes or study aids while you complete the assessment.

It is vital that you know and write enough to pass the Unit Assessments as you will not be awarded a Higher in Business Management unless you do. Even if you score 100% in the final exam the award will be withheld until you achieve a pass in each internal Unit Assessment.

If you are struggling to pass the Unit Assessment it might well be an indication that you are studying at the wrong level and should consider moving to Intermediate 2 Business Management.

The Unit Assessments come from a **N**ational **A**ssessment **B**ank and so are often referred to as NABs.

GETTING NABed!

The Unit Assessments consist of questions based on a case study of a real business. Your teacher might well give the case study out a few days before you are NABed. This will give you time to study it. You will be given a fresh copy of the case study at the time of the assessment to ensure no one tries to take any notes into the test.

The case study is not really that long – about 300 words. Getting it out early will give you a chance to focus on the areas you might be tested on.

 If your teacher gives you the case study early use the time wisely to consider what type of things might be asked in the Unit Assessment.

The Unit Assessments (NABs) will draw questions from a specific part of the syllabus. The final examination will assess elements from the whole course.

The questions are straightforward. They are not designed to trick you. Make sure to take account of the command words when answering the questions and also mirror your answer on the number of marks awarded – generally one mark will be awarded for each valid point given. Some questions ask for general examples to be given and these will be awarded with marks. Remember, the NAB is really there to enable you to demonstrate that you understand the essential aspects of Business Management that you have studied in a Unit and to apply your knowledge and understanding to answer the questions fully.

 See Chapter 1 for information on command words.

This might well be your first timed assessment at Higher level and so time management is crucial if you are to achieve your potential. The questions in the Unit Assessments are not too different to the type of questions found in past paper questions so you can use these to practise.

Throughout the year you will have three Unit Assessments to sit for Higher Business Management. Each assessment lasts a maximum of 60 minutes. All three Unit Assessments are worth a total of 40 marks and you need to achieve at least 50% or 20 of the available 40 marks to pass. If you practise you should have no problem achieving a pass.

The NAB itself will contain a mixture of Short Answer Questions and Extended Response Questions.

Short Answer Questions are there to allow you to show understanding of terminology, e.g. **name**, **identify**. However, these simpler types of questions will usually only account for a maximum of 6 marks throughout the whole paper. On the other hand, Extended Response Questions are there to provide you with the opportunity to develop and explain points of Business Management you have studied in the Unit in your answers, e.g. **describe**, **justify**, **explain**, and will account for about 20 marks. Finally there will be some Extended Response Questions which require even more skill and understanding, e.g. **discuss** or **compare**, and these question account for the balance of marks available (about 14). The questions are based on the case study, so make sure you thoroughly read and understand it. You often have to answer in context making specific reference to the case study.

Never aim for the minimum pass mark but always try your best to score as many marks as possible. These Unit Assessments will help prepare you for your final SQA examination in the summer.

 During the assessment, if you do not know the answer to one question simply move onto the next one and hopefully there will be time to come back and attempt the question later.

For all three NABs you must be able to give reasons/justifications for any conclusions you state in your answers and use relevant concepts from Business Management in your analysis of the questions/problems posed.

High scoring evidence (not a 50% pass mark) from Unit Assessments may be used to support an appeal should you not achieve the grade expected in the final exam – but only in exceptional circumstances. It can never be the only evidence used to support your appeal but it can sometimes help build up a picture of your capability and may add weight to other evidence submitted, such as a Prelim paper.

Some specifics to help you prepare for your Unit Assessments

In the Unit Assessments you will answer between five and six questions. Each of the questions will cover only one area of the Unit but be aware that because this particular section is so large and varied, the questions may jump about. For example, one question might look at the *Objectives* of a business while the next question could jump to *Decision Making*.

The questions can only hope to sample the areas you have studied. There is no way of telling what is going to be asked and so you should use the Unit Assessments for preparation for the final examination – where you have no idea what areas will be covered.

Let's put some of what we have just read to some use by doing some practice NABs for Business Enterprise.

FIRST

🖎 Read the case study and try to work out how it applies to what you have studied for this Unit.

SECOND

🖎 Look at the questions and try to answer them – I know this will be very hard to do without looking at the suggested answers but go on, give it a go.

THEN

🖎 Look at the suggested answers and compare them with what you have written.

Most books on Business Management give solutions to questions. Beware – they are usually in the form of bulleted points which you will have to be clever enough to expand when doing Unit Assessments OR your final SQA examination.

PRACTICE TIME

Unit 1 – Business Enterprise

The Unit Assessment covers **three** areas of the course.

❶ *Business in Contemporary Society*

☑ Role of business in society

☑ Types of business organisations

☑ Objectives of business

☑ Role of the enterprise and the entrepreneur

☑ Stakeholders

☑ Factors affecting the operation of business

☑ Business as a dynamic activity

❷ *Business Information and IT*

☑ Sources of information

☑ Types of information

☑ Value of information

☑ ICT in business

❸ *Decision Making in Business*

☑ Decision making

☑ Decision making model

☑ SWOT analysis

☑ Problems with structured models

🖎 Note that the last area of Business Enterprise – Internal Organisation – is not tested in the Unit Assessments.

Business Enterprise – Practice Assessment 1

Read the following case study on Ninewells Hospital in Dundee.

Ninewells Hospital is situated on the western edge of Dundee and operates as part of NHS Tayside.

The accident and emergency unit deals with 55,000 admissions – including 3,500 broken bones, 150 heart attacks and 20,000 X-rays. In addition to the hospital, there is a teaching section that includes the medical school and nursing school of the University of Dundee. As such it was the second purpose-built medical school in the UK.

Ninewells Hospital strives to ensure that it meets the high standards expected of those who use its services. The hospital 'benchmarks' itself against government data on waiting times for patients to receive treatment and the infection rates in other NHS hospitals around the UK. Personal satisfaction is checked with random sampling of individual patients who are asked to complete a questionnaire on their experiences in the hospital.

The hospital was built on to the side of a hill and the practicalities of the design were influenced by airport check-in. Phase I of the building was completed in 1973, although some sections were not finished until 1975. The final cost from government funding was £25 million. Hospital admittances started in January 1974 and the hospital was officially opened by the Queen Mother on October 23, 1974. At the opening ceremony, she stated '... *nothing that science can devise, nor money provide, will be lacking for the treatment of the patients'*.

Maggie's Centre at Ninewells Hospital

The Board of Trustees, who administer the hospital, felt that there was a need in Tayside to better support children who had been diagnosed with cancer. This led to the commissioning of architects Frank Gehry and James F. Stephen to design a purpose-built facility in the grounds of Ninewells Hospital. Maggie's Centre, as it was to be known, was officially opened by Bob Geldof in 2003.

Now attempt to answer the following questions. Try timing yourself to see if you can complete the questions in 60 minutes.

Sample answers can be found at the end – remember don't sneak a look until you've tried answering the questions first.

1 (a) Name the business sector that Ninewells Hospital operates in. Justify your answer. (2 marks)

   (b) Discuss the benefits of the hospital operating in this business sector. (6 marks)

2 State three different objectives Ninewells Hospital could have and describe how they can be met. (6 marks)

3 Explain the influence stakeholders have on a hospital. (3 marks)

4 Compare Ninewells Hospital to Tesco plc in terms of ownership, control and finance. (3 marks)

5 (a) From the text, identify one example of a strategic, a tactical and an operational decision that has been made by Ninewells Hospital. Justify your choice of examples. (6 marks)

   (b) Ninewells Hospital might well have made use of a structured decision making model when making decisions. Discuss the use of such models. (5 marks)

6 Technology plays a vital part in communication in a large hospital such as Ninewells.

   (a) Outline ICT that can be used to ensure effective communication in a large hospital. (4 marks)

   (b) Discuss the effectiveness of ICT as a means of communication. (5 marks)

Have you checked your answers?

Ready for another case study?

Business Enterprise – Practice Assessment 2

Read the following case study on the pharmaceutical company
GlaxoSmithKline (GSK).

 GlaxoSmithKline (GSK) plc was
formed by the merger of Glaxo
Wellcome (formed from the mergers
of Burroughs Wellcome & Company
and Glaxo Laboratories), and
SmithKline Beecham (from Beecham, and SmithKline Bechman).

GSK's head office is in London. It is one of the industry leaders, with
an estimated 7% of the world's pharmaceutical market. The company
achieved sales of £22.7 billion and made a profit of £7.8 billion in 2007.

The company is listed on the London and New York stock exchanges.

As a company with firm foundations in science, it has a flair for research
and a track record of turning that research into powerful, marketable
drugs. Every hour GSK spends more than £300,000 on developing
new medicines.

Research is carried out by GSK in the South of England where clinical
tests or drug trials are carried out to determine the effectiveness of new
medicines. GSK also benefits from international cooperation from fellow
pharmaceutical companies who share ideas to find cures for conditions
such as HIV.

The company produces medicines that treat six major disease areas –
asthma, virus control, infections, mental health, diabetes and digestive
conditions. In addition, GSK is a leader in the important area of vaccines
and is developing new treatments for cancer.

GSK employs around 110,000 people worldwide with production sites in
Irvine and Montrose showing its commitment to the Scottish economy.

Recently GSK reviewed its worldwide manufacturing operations.
This resulted in a decision to rationalise production by transfering
the manufacturing of key pharmaceuticals from sites in Scotland. In
Montrose this left the company with the difficult task of deciding who to
offer redundancy packages to as the site halved its workforce.

GSK was named one of the 100 Best Companies for Working Mothers in
2007 by *Working Mother* magazine.

Now attempt to answer the following questions. Try timing yourself to see if you can complete the questions in 60 minutes.

Sample answers can be found at the end – remember don't sneak a look until you've tried answering the questions first.

---

1 (a) Identify the type of business organisation described in the case study. Justify your answer.

(2 marks)

(b) Explain the advantages of this type of business structure. (4 marks)

2 GSK requires vast sums of funding to research new medicines. Describe three ways GSK could fund this research. (3 marks)

3 Outline the interest and influence three stakeholders have on GSK. (6 marks)

4 Compare three objectives of GSK to those of the BBC.

(3 marks)

5 GSK rationalised production.

(a) From the text, identify a strategic, a tactical and an operational decision which supported this aim. Justify your examples. (6 marks)

(b) Outline how GSK could use a structured decision making model in this process. (5 marks)

6 GSK obtains information from primary and secondary sources. Identify one example of each type of information and justify its reliability. (4 marks)

7 GSK is a multinational corporation.

(a) Explain how technology can be used to communicate between international sites. (4 marks)

(b) Discuss possible disadvantages regarding the use of modern technology. (3 marks)

Unit 2 – Business Decision Areas: Marketing and Operations

The Unit Assessment covers **two** areas of the course.

❶ *Marketing*

- ☑ Marketing
- ☑ The marketing concept
- ☑ The marketing mix
- ☑ Target markets
- ☑ Market research

❷ *Operations*

- ☑ Operations
- ☑ Input, process and output
- ☑ Distribution and delivery
- ☑ Types of operations
- ☑ Quality

Business Decision Areas: Marketing and Operations – Practice Assessment

Read the following case study on Simple.

The Company

Simple is a Californian based corporation, solely distributed in the UK by an Inverclyde company with a strong ethical stance. In response to what they saw as an over marketing of shoes they formed Simple in 1991 with a desire to promote environmentally friendly marketing and operation practices.

With all the over-built, over-hyped products out there, Simple felt that it was hard to find an eco-friendly shoe that is both stylish and kind to the environment. The company recognised that they were targeting a niche market but one which they believed was growing.

Their commitment to the environment involves recycling car tyres and plastic bottles in the production process. In 2006 they reduced their packaging to the bare minimum. Packaging became 100% recyclable.

Simple even produce a range of shoes that are Vegan friendly – using no animal products.

The Process

The large range of shoes offered by Simple means that the company operates a batch production system. The company is relatively small and so stock levels are carefully monitored to ensure that excess funds are not tied up in the warehouse. At the same time Simple realise that customers should not be kept waiting for orders.

Simple started by using sustainable materials (*raw materials that can easily be replaced*), e.g. bamboo which grows at 20 feet a year is used for manufacturing heels. This replaced traditional materials such as jute, a much slower growing crop. The soles of many of Simple's shoes are made from old tyres and the uppers from recycled plastic bottles.

'*Sometimes our progress is notable while at other times the improvements are harder to come by. The important thing is we're committed to making our product 100% sustainable. Finding materials and processes that make our products sustainable is a method we call Green Toe.*'

Quote from website

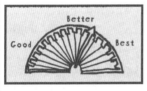

Progress in Green Toe is measured with a scale called 'good, better, best.' The best category represents the most sustainable shoes and sets the bar for the rest of the line. These same innovative materials and constructions can be found in the good and better categories, raising the bar for the best products.

Source: Adapted from www.simpleshoes.com

Now attempt to answer the following questions. Try timing yourself to see if you can complete the questions in 60 minutes.

Sample answers can be found at the end – remember don't sneak a look until you've tried answering the questions first.

1	Justify the role played by Marketing in organisations.	(3 marks)
2	(i) Explain the importance of the elements in the marketing mix for Simple.	(4 marks)
	(ii) Describe how elements of the marketing mix identified in (i) relate to one another.	(3 marks)
3	Simple recognise that they are targeting a 'niche market'.	
	(i) Explain the benefits of niche marketing.	(3 marks)
	(ii) Identify general market segments for Simple.	(3 marks)
4	(i) Explain one way of carrying out desk research and one way of carrying out field research.	(2 marks)
	(ii) Describe one advantage of desk research and one advantage of field research.	(2 marks)
5	Explain the importance of the purchasing mix for a business like Simple.	(4 marks)
6	Simple uses batch production. Compare this method of production with other methods of production.	(4 marks)
7	Simple keeps stock levels to a minimum. Describe the considerations that need to be considered in arriving at stock levels.	(4 marks)
8	Green Toe is a method by which Simple hope to improve the quality of their products.	
	(i) Other than Green Toe, justify additional ways Simple could improve quality.	(4 marks)
	(ii) Describe costs which could be associated with the introduction of a quality system.	(2 marks)
9	Simple sell around the world through its website and stores. Explain two external factors which might prevent Simple from delivering their products to customers.	(2 marks)

Unit 3 – Business Decision Areas: Finance and Human Resource Management

The Unit Assessment covers **two** areas of the course.

❶ *Financial Management*

☑ Finance

☑ Financial information

☑ Cash flow management

☑ Budgetary control

☑ Ratio analysis

❷ *Human Resource Management*

☑ Human resource management

☑ Changing pattern of employment within organisations

☑ Recruitment and selection

☑ Training and development

☑ Employee relations

☑ Legislative requirements

Business Decision Areas: Finance and Human Resource Management – Practice Assessment

Read the following case study on the Bank of Scotland.

The Bank of Scotland is the UK's oldest commercial bank, created by an Act of the Scottish Parliament in 1695.

HBOS was formed by the 2001 merger of the Halifax plc and the Bank of Scotland, creating the fifth-largest bank in the UK. It became a very successful company as the UK's largest mortgage provider.

Problems arose for HBOS with the emergence of an economic downturn in 2008 which left them vulnerable to cash-flow problems.

From being a highly successful company, profits began to tumble. HBOS, which had made a £5.5-billion pre-tax profit in 2007, reported a £10.8-billion pre-tax loss in 2008.

A growing economic crisis lead the Prime Minister, Gordon Brown, in October 2008 to announce a government capital-bailout to HBOS of £11.5 billion. This resulted in the government taking ownership of 40% of HBOS.

HBOS were not alone in their difficulties; many other financial companies were experiencing severe cash-flow problems. One bank, Northern Rock, suffered such a liquidity crisis that the government had to bail them out with huge sums of public money. The economic downturn sent the share prices of many banks into freefall. The government felt forced to buy a 65% share in HBOS's Scottish rival, RBS, when a new share issue failed to attract interest from investors.

HBOS sought security with a merger with Lloyds TSB in January 2009 to create a 'superbank' with 38 million customers.

The merger resulted in a review of management structures. The historic name of Scotland's oldest bank survived with all high street branches trading under the Bank of Scotland brand. The banks stated that the new group would continue to use the 'The Mound' in Edinburgh as the headquarters for the Scottish operation and would continue to issue Scottish bank notes.

The coming together of two similar institutions had an effect on jobs. The merger resulted in the duplication of departments, managers and staff. Staff lost their jobs, others volunteered to retrain for other posts in the new structure.

In the future, unions fear there may be a need to close branches resulting in yet more redundancies. Some estimate that job losses could be as high as 14,000. In a highly competitive market there is also the concern that services will be off-shored where wages are cheaper.

Now attempt to answer the following questions. Try timing yourself to see if you can complete the questions in 60 minutes.

Sample answers can be found at the end – remember don't sneak a look until you've tried answering the questions first.

---

1 Explain the role of the Finance Department in a large organisation like the Bank of Scotland. (4 marks)

2 (i) Identify one accounting ratio used to measure profitability and one ratio to measure liquidity. (2 marks)

   (ii) Describe ways in which profitability and liquidity in the ratios identified in (i) could be improved. (2 marks)

   (iii) Discuss why financial information should not be the only measure of an organisation's potential. (3 marks)

3 Describe and justify the importance of the following accounting terms:
   Cash flow
   Assets
   Liabilities (6 marks)

4 Justify the use of budgets in organisations. (3 marks)

5 Explain the specific roles of HRM in a large organisation like the Bank of Scotland. (5 marks)

6 The Bank of Scotland was created by an Act of Parliament in 1695.

Explain more recent forms of legislation referring to HRM. (3 marks)

7 'Off-shoring' is the transfer of services abroad. This involves the recruitment of staff in those countries.

Describe stages in an effective recruitment and selection process. (6 marks)

8 A function of the HRM Department is to support staff training.

Discuss advantages and disadvantages of staff training. (6 marks)

SAMPLE ANSWERS TO CASE STUDIES

NINEWELLS HOSPITAL – SOLUTIONS

Some solutions show brackets ( ) – this means that the mark can be gained without those particular words BUT the answer is enhanced by it.

1 (a) Name the business sector that Ninewells Hospital operates in. Justify your answer.

Ninewells Hospital operates in the public sector. (1 mark) This is clear because it is (part of the NHS and is) funded by the government. (1 mark)

(b) Discuss the benefits of the hospital operating in this business sector.

Public sector organisations benefit from local or centralised government funding to support their operations. This means that they are not as vulnerable to market conditions as private sector business. (1 mark) They could however find themselves facing financial cutbacks due to reduced government funding. (1 mark)

While there is some degree of competition in the form of private hospitals, competition is limited. (1 mark) Because profit-maximisation is not an objective, public sector organisations can focus on the quality of service. (1 mark)

The hospital is able to provide a service that would be out of the financial reach of all but a few members of the public. (1 mark)

Public sector organisations are often accused of being bureaucratic or top heavy making them inefficient, as they are slow to change or react. (1 mark)

2 State three different objectives Ninewells Hospital could have and describe how they can be met.

Provision of a quality service. (1 mark) This could be achieved by employing highly qualified staff and investing in modern equipment. (1 mark)

Expansion of services/growth. (1 mark) The hospital could open new wards specialising in different areas (for example eating disorders like anorexia or bulimia). (1 mark)

Breaking-even. (1 mark) The hospital may encourage fund-raising events to support the work of the hospital. (1 mark)

3 Explain the influence stakeholders have on a hospital.

The Board of Trustees (managers) make strategic decisions regarding allocation of funds in the hospital. (1 mark) Doctors/nurses/physiotherapists (employees) influence the hospital by the standard of their work. (1 mark) Patients (customers) have the ultimate power as to whether to use the hospital or not. (1 mark)

The number of marks indicates the number of points you have to give. This particular question is worth three marks, indicating that you need to mention the influence of <u>three</u> separate stakeholders or <u>three</u> influences of one stakeholder.

4 Compare Ninewells Hospital to Tesco plc in terms of ownership, control and finance.

Ninewells Hospital is owned by the public whereas Tesco plc is owned by the shareholders. (1 mark) The control of Ninewells is carried out by the Board of Trustees however control of a plc is by the Board of Directors. (1 mark) Ninewells Hospital is a public sector organisation and as such is funded by the government through taxation. On the other hand Tesco is a public limited company and as such is funded through share issue and profits. (1 mark)

When answering a question where you are asked to make a comparison on more than one factor it is a good idea to use connecting words/phrases such as ... *however,* ... *both,* ... *whereas,* ... *but, this is not* ..., ... *on the other hand.*

Take care with solutions that show answers in the form of a table – they are shown like this for ease of understanding and not for copying in an exam.

5 (a) From the text, identify one example each of a strategic, a tactical and an operational decision that has been made by Ninewells Hospital. Justify your choice of examples.

A strategic decision is for the hospital to offer better care for children with cancer. (1 mark) This is strategic because it is long-term and made by senior management. (1 mark)

A tactical decision is the appointment of Frank Gehry and James F. Stephen as architects. (1 mark) This is tactical because it supports the strategic decision above. (1 mark)

An operational decision might be which patients to sample with a questionnaire. (1 mark) This decision is operational because is not a very significant decision – it is also likely to be made by junior managers e.g. reception staff. (1 mark)

When asked to 'justify' use the word 'because'.

(b) **Ninewells Hospital might well have made use of a structured decision making model when making decisions. Discuss the use of such models.**

A structured decision making model will result in a more considered decision since time will be taken to go through each stage. (1 mark) Each stage of a structured decision making model supports the next step leading to better decision making. (1 mark)

Any structured decision making model is time consuming and this is a major drawback. (1 mark) No matter how detailed a model is it cannot take account of all factors in arriving at a decision and there are still likely to be considerations that have not been taken into account. (1 mark)

Structured decision making models are often accused of stifling creativity – the gut feeling of managers – which are often seen as the best reactions. (1 mark)

'Discuss' requires an account of strengths and weaknesses. Do not feel that you have to provide equal numbers of each in an answer.

6   **Technology plays a vital part in communication in a large hospital such as Ninewells.**

(a) **Outline ICT that can be used to ensure effective communication in a large hospital.**

Networks, either Local Area Networks (LAN) or Wide Area Networks (WAN), can be used to connect computer terminals. (1 mark) Pagers would be an effective way of contacting medical staff when they are urgently needed. (1 mark) Email is used in most organisations to pass on communication as messages are sent almost instantly (and can be sent to more than one person at a time). (1 mark) Videoconferencing could be used to allow meetings to be held with people from various sites around the country or abroad. (Visiting lecturers could also provide lectures to the medical and nursing school.) (1 mark)

(b) Discuss the effectiveness of ICT as a means of communication.

ICT allows information to be transmitted far quicker than conventional means resulting in increased efficiency. (1 mark)

ICT allows staff to get in touch with each other while working away from a traditional means of communication such as a landline. (1 mark)

The cost of purchasing and updating ICT can be prohibitive (1 mark) and staff may need training. (1 mark)

The ease by which information can be sent with ICT can result in unnecessary communication that slows down effectiveness. (There are studies that show that staff constantly check emails at the cost of more productive work.) (1 mark)

The above answers are not exhaustive, they simply illustrate the type of responses that could gain marks. If you come up with other answers ask your teacher to check that they are worth a mark.

GLAXOSMITHKLINE (GSK) – SOLUTIONS

Some solutions show brackets ( ) – this means that the mark can be gained without those particular words BUT the answer is enhanced by it.

1 (a) Identify the type of business organisation described in the case study. Justify your answer.

GSK is a public limited company. (1 mark) This is evident from the 'plc' after its name (and the statement claiming it is listed on the London and New York stock exchanges). (1 mark)

 Look out for more than one command word in a question. The amount of marks available for a question should also alert you to the number of points to give in your answer.

(b) Explain the advantages of this type of business structure.

Liability for the shareholders/owners is limited to the amount they invest in the business. This will encourage funds as investors will be happier that they are not putting their personal belongings at risk. (1 mark)

Plcs tend to be large organisations and they usually find it easier to get finance. Banks feel the loan is more secure because plcs usually have more assets that can be sold if they default on the loan. (1 mark)

Because of their size they can sometimes control the market. This can allow them to set a high price. (1 mark)

Again because of size, plcs can benefit from economies of scale. Selling large volumes can make it cheaper for the business to buy its own transport division than use an independent company. (1 mark)

2 GSK requires vast sums of funding to research new medicines. Describe three ways GSK could fund this research.

Debentures are loans that are only available to public limited companies. They allow for large funds to be received and only interest paid back until some future time when the loan itself is repaid. (1 mark)

Retained profits, that is profits not given out to shareholders in the form of dividends, could be used to support research. (Profits of £7.8 billion in 2007.) (1 mark)

GSK could sell more shares on the stock market. Since GSK is a profitable company they should find it easy to generate money in this way. (1 mark)

3 Outline the interest and influence three stakeholders have on GSK.

Scientists are stakeholders in GSK and (as employees) they are **interested** in job security, good wages and promotion prospects. (1 mark) The creativity and ingenuity of the many scientists who work for GSK **influences** the development of new pharmaceuticals that can be very profitable to the company. (1 mark)

Shareholders are also stakeholders and (as owners) they are looking for or are **interested** in a return on their investment in the form of dividends. (1 mark) Shareholders are **influential** stakeholders because they have voting rights at the AGM to appoint the Board of Directors (other stakeholders) who will make the decisions concerning operations. (1 mark)

The government is a stakeholder who wants or is **interested** in most business organisations being successful because they reduce unemployment, resulting in the government paying out less in benefits and receiving more in income tax. (1 mark) The government's **influence(s)** lies in its ability to set levels of taxation which will affect the amount of funds that are ultimately at the disposal of GSK for new and existing projects. (1 mark)

If you are answering a question on the influence of stakeholders make sure you do not simply state why they are stakeholders. 'Interest' is what is in it for them – 'influence' is about power.

Also notice that there are no marks for identification of stakeholders – this is normal at Higher level – marks are given for their interest and their influence.

4   Compare three objectives of GSK to those of the BBC.

The main objective of GSK is likely to be profit maximisation to provide healthy dividends to shareholders whereas the BBC's aim is to keep within the budget allocated by the government. (1 mark)

Another GSK objective could be growth through further mergers or takeovers whereas the BBC might want to grow by offering more services, e.g. programmes, but they are not likely to want to grow through joining with other broadcasting corporations. (1 mark)

Both organisations want to be innovative. The BBC through cutting edge programmes whereas GSK want to provide treatments to diseases that are at present incurable. (1 mark)

When comparing use 'whereas' to ensure that a comparison is being made.

5   GSK rationalised production.

(a)   From the text, identify a strategic, a tactical and an operational decision which supported this aim. Justify your examples.

A strategic decision was to review its worldwide manufacturing operations. (1 mark) This is a general decision – non-specific – without detail and made by top management. (1 mark)

A tactical decision was to move some of the production from Scotland. (1 mark) This is more specific than the previous decision. It adds detail. (1 mark)

An operational decision would be who to make redundant. (1 mark) This supports the previous tactical decision and is very specific. (1 mark)

(b) Outline how GSK could use a structured decision making model in this process.

GSK should identify the objectives to be achieved from rationalising production, e.g. increased efficiency. (1 mark) They should then gather information, e.g. profitability or capacity of GSK's production sites. (1 mark)

Once this has been done they should analyse the information gathered, e.g. make comparisons. (1 mark) After analysis, they will then devise alternative solutions, e.g. prepare a short list of potential sites which would have production curtailed. (1 mark)

Finally GSK will select from alternative solutions, i.e. decide on the sites to be affected. (1 mark)

 The first stage of a structured decision making model is to identify the problem. In most questions however the 'problem' will already have been stated and so no mark will be given for the first stage.

6 GSK obtains information from primary and secondary sources. Identify one example of each type of information and justify its reliability.

Primary information from clinical tests or drug trials. (1 mark)

Secondary information from sharing ideas with other pharmaceutical companies. (1 mark)

The primary source is likely to be reliable because GSK have control over its collection. (1 mark)

However no guarantees can be made of the secondary information as GSK has no first-hand knowledge of its reliability. (1 mark)

7 GSK is a multinational corporation.

(a) Explain how technology can be used to communicate between international sites.

Email is an efficient method of passing on information as it can be transmitted almost instantly around the world. (1 mark) One message can be sent to several recipients at the same time. (1 mark)

Videoconferencing is a way of conducting meetings/presentations without the need to travel. Staff can see and speak to each other via a video link. (1 mark)

Wide Area Network (WAN) will allow access to secure information located on a server. (1 mark)

Notice that two marks can be awarded for the same form of technology providing you make two different points.

(b) Discuss possible disadvantages regarding the use of modern technology.

Modern technology is open to viruses which can corrupt data. (1 mark) Another issue regarding modern technology is that staff usually need training in its use in the workplace. (1 mark) Also there are often major costs in purchasing technology. (1 mark)

The above answers are not exhaustive, they simply illustrate the type of responses that could gain marks. If you come up with other answers ask your teacher to check that they are worth a mark.

SIMPLE SHOES – SOLUTIONS

Some solutions show brackets ( ) – this means that the mark can be gained without those particular words BUT the answer is enhanced by it.

1 Justify the role played by marketing in organisations.

A role of marketing is to publicise product(s) or service(s). Failure to do this will result in few customers. (1 mark)

Failure to take account of customer needs – found through marketing research – will mean that organisations will fail to achieve their objectives, e.g. profit maximisation for a restaurant or new members for a social club. (1 mark)

Another role of marketing is to anticipate future needs and if this is not done then demand is likely to decline/disappear forcing the organisation out of business. (1 mark)

Notice that to answer the above question it is necessary to 'identify' the role of Marketing and yet no marks are awarded for this. The marks are awarded for 'justifying' its importance.

Appreciate that Marketing is equally vital to public sector and charitable organisations as to private sector businesses.

2 (i) Explain the importance of the elements of the marketing mix for Simple.

Price – this is how much Simple charge for their shoes. This must be set at a level that covers costs and takes account of competitors' prices. (1 mark)

Place – this is how the customer can access the shoes – in the case of Simple this is through their website and stores. This element is fundamental to sales and generating revenue. (1 mark)

Product – this is the actual shoes. Simple have a relatively unique aspect to their shoes in that they aim to be made of sustainable materials appealing to their niche market. (1 mark)

Promotion – is how customers are persuaded to buy their products. Simple must persuade their customers to buy their shoes. (1 mark)

(ii) Describe how elements of the marketing mix identified in (i) relate to one another.

Product and **Price** are related in that a product that is expensive to produce will need to be sold at a high price to cover costs. (1 mark)

The **Price** charged for a product often has to rise to cover the money spent on costly advertising (**Promotion**). (1 mark)

A **Product** aimed at a particular market needs to be **Promoted** where that market will notice. In the case of Simple, the new vegan range could be advertised in vegan magazines. (1 mark)

3 Simple recognise that they are targeting a 'niche market'.

(i) Explain the benefits of niche marketing.

When a niche market is targeted then that small group of consumers get exactly what they want. (There is no need to compromise on their wants.) (1 mark)

Customers are specifically targeted through promotion and so they are well aware of the existence of the product/service. (1 mark)

Niche markets tend to lack competition and so suppliers of such markets can often command high prices for their goods/services. (1 mark)

 Niche marketing can have advantages for the consumer and the supplier.

(ii) Identify general market segments for Simple.

Simple could target males or females depending on the type of footwear they produce. (1 mark)

The company strives to be ecologically aware and this is communicated through its publicity. It would therefore be likely to aim its shoes at those who are educated. (1 mark)

By charging a high price for their goods Simple could aim their products at people with a high disposable income. (1 mark)

4 (i) Explain one way for Simple to carry out desk research and one way of carrying out field research.

Desk research: using the internet to look at the websites of similar suppliers will allow Simple to compare prices and product ranges with competitors. (1 mark)

Field research: carrying out personal interviews through questionnaires with a sample of the public will allow Simple to gauge demand. (1 mark)

 Note that there's no mark for simply naming a form of desk and field research.

(ii) Describe one advantage of desk research and one advantage of field research.

Desk research: is less time-consuming since the information is often already to hand and does not need to be produced. (1 mark)

Field research: this information can be kept private since the collector is more likely to own the information and therefore have control of its use. (1 mark)

 Often an advantage of one method is a disadvantage of another.

5 Explain the importance of the purchasing mix for a business like Simple.

Quality raw materials are likely to lead to a quality end product. (1 mark)

The choice of a reliable supplier will determine whether Simple can meet its own commitments to customers. (1 mark)

The price charged by suppliers and credit terms are important considerations for any business and can adversely affect cashflow. (1 mark)

Storage of raw materials is a major cost for manufactures like Simple. (1 mark)

6 Simple uses batch production.

Compare this method of production with other methods of production.

Batch production involves the production of relatively small amounts of one product before changing production to the manufacture of another; whereas flow/line production involves the large-scale continuous production of one identical product. (1 mark)

Like flow/line production, batch production tends to be capital intensive unlike job production which tends to be labour intensive. (1 mark)

Batch production allows a degree of change in the final product to suit the individual needs of customers while flow/line production produces a uniformed end product. (1 mark)

Batch production can result in savings due to economies of scale. Job production is unable to take advantage of economies of scale due to the individual nature of the end product. (1 mark)

When answering a question where you are asked to make a comparison on more than one factor it is a good idea to use connecting words/phrases such as … *however,* … *both,* … *whereas,* … *but,* … *unlike, this is not …,* … *on the other hand.*

Take care with solutions that show answers in the form of a table – they are shown like this for ease of understanding and not for copying in an exam.

7 Simple keeps stock levels to a minimum.

Describe the considerations that need to be considered in arriving at stock levels.

Maximum stock levels ensure that production will be uninterrupted. Consideration should be given to the cost of storage and the possibility of spoilage. (1 mark)

Reordering stock level is the point at which falling stock levels trigger the recording of more stock, taking account of delivery times from suppliers. (1 mark)

Reorder quantity is the amount necessary, taking account of usage during delivery times, that will push the stock level back up to the maximum stock level. (1 mark)

Minimum stock level acts as a buffer to ensure that production does not stop. It is important that stock is ordered/delivered on time to prevent the minimum level being breached. (1 mark)

 The use of a well labelled diagram such as this one showing stock levels will gain 1 or 2 marks.

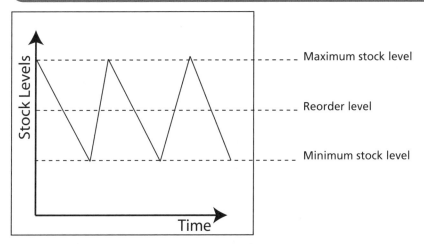

8   **Green Toe is a method by which Simple hope to improve the quality of their products.**

(i)   **Other than Green Toe, justify additional ways Simple could improve quality.**

Purchase of quality raw materials should result in less waste and better quality shoes. (Better inputs result in better outputs.) (1 mark)

Training the workforce/employing skilled workers should result in fewer defects. (1 mark)

Quality control, normally at the end of the production process, ensures that the product will be fit for purpose. (1 mark)

Total Quality Management (TQM), where everyone is responsible for quality, should make sure that defective work is corrected before it goes on to the next stage of the production process. (1 mark)

(ii) Describe costs which could be associated with the introduction of a quality system.

Cost of training, or the higher wages paid to attract skilled staff, would be an obvious cost. (1 mark)

Any new system such as QC or TQM would need to have procedures and paperwork drawn up. (Meetings would have to be held to discuss the best practice.) (1 mark)

9 Simple sell around the world through its website and stores.

Explain two external factors which might prevent Simple from delivering their products to customers.

Bad weather could mean that deliveries are unable to get through to customers. (1 mark)

Problems with suppliers of raw materials would hold back production levels making it impossible for Simple to honour orders. (1 mark)

The above answers are not exhaustive, they simply illustrate the type of responses that could gain marks. If you come up with other answers ask your teacher to check that they are worth a mark.

THE BANK OF SCOTLAND – SOLUTIONS

Some solutions show brackets ( ) – this means that the mark can be gained without those particular words BUT the answer is enhanced by it.

1 Explain the role of the Finance Department in a large organisation like the Bank of Scotland.

Preparation of financial statements, such as Trading, Profit and Loss Accounts and Balance Sheets, to report on an organisation's activities. (1 mark)

The Finance Department will collect and process financial information to allow managers to make informed decisions. (1 mark)

The role of the Finance Department is to record the flow of funds to alert managers to problems before they become too serious. (1 mark)

Ensure that funds are available (such as arranging loans, agreeing credit terms) to make sure that the organisation can achieve its objectives. (1 mark)

 With an 'explain' question you often have to give a reason. Use words or phrases such as *so that* …, …*because, to* … This will ensure that you are actually explaining.

2 (i) Identify one accounting ratio used to measure profitability and one ratio to measure liquidity.

Net Profit ratio
(Profitability)

$\dfrac{\text{Net Profit}}{\text{Sales/Turnover}}$ %

(1 mark)

Current ratio
(Liquidity)

Current assets : Current liabilities

(1 mark)

(ii) Describe ways in which profitability and liquidity in the ratios identified in (i) could be improved.

Reduce expenses such as changing energy provider (for example British Gas to Hydro Electric or vice versa) would result in greater profits. (1 mark)

Retaining more funds in either bank or cash (current assets) in relation to the current liabilities would improve liquidity. (1 mark)

(iii) Discuss why financial information should not be the only measure of an organisation's potential.

Financial information provides objective information based on fact. (1 mark)

Information is often historic and does not reflect what might happen in the future. (1 mark)

It does not take account of non-financial factors such as strength of the management team, enthusiasm/dedication of staff. (1 mark)

 Discuss questions look for strengths and weaknesses. It is not necessary to have equal numbers of each.

3 Describe and justify the importance of the following accounting terms:

Cash flow

Assets

Liabilities

Cash flow represents the amount of funds flowing through an organisation. (1 mark) At any one point in time, where the amount flowing out is greater than the amount coming in then the organisation could be forced to stop trading. (1 mark)

Assets are the items owned by the organisation (they may be fixed or current). (An example of a fixed asset is 'premises' and an example of a current asset is 'stock'.) (1 mark) Assets support the operations of an organisation. If organisations did not have assets they would not be able to carryout their activities and meet their objectives. (1 mark)

Liabilities are owed by the business. (1 mark) They improve the cash flow in an organisation by deferring payments (e.g. Creditors) or obtaining funds (loans/overdraft/mortgage/debentures). (1 mark)

4   **Justify the use of budgets in organisations.**

Budgets compare actual performance with projected to highlight discrepancies. (1 mark)

They set targets which will motivate/focus staff. (1 mark)

Budgets are delegated to staff/departments to encourage responsibility. (1 mark)

5   **Explain the specific roles of HRM in a large organisation like the Bank of Scotland.**

Facilitating role – providing training to other departments to support Human Resource Management. (1 mark)

Auditing role – checking practices and procedures to ensure they follow the standards set by the Human Resource Department. (1 mark)

Consultancy role – being available to staff for advice and guidance. (1 mark)

Executive role – this is a management role equal to other management roles in an organisation. (1 mark)

Service role – responsible for ensuring that the organisation is kept up-to-date with current practices including legislation. (1 mark)

6   **The Bank of Scotland was created by an Act of Parliament in 1695.**

Explain more recent forms of legislation referring to HRM.

Sex Discrimination Act has implications on the recruitment, promotion and training of staff in that males and females are to be treated equally. (1 mark)

Health and Safety at Work Act lays a responsibility on employers and employees to ensure that the workplace is free of unnecessary hazards and dangers. (1 mark)

Data Protection Act requires HRM departments to ensure that information on staff is accurate, relevant, secure and available for inspection by the individual member of staff. (1 mark)

Be guided by the number of marks as to the number of points you need to give.

Don't try to remember the dates of Acts.

7 ***'Off-shoring'* is the transfer of services abroad. This involves the recruitment of staff in those countries.**

Describe the stages in an effective recruitment and selection process.

Carry out a Job Analysis to find out if the job should be filled. This can be used to identify skills necessary to carry out the job. (An organisation might decide not to continue beyond this stage if there is no evidence that a job is necessary.) (1 mark)

Prepare a Job Description detailing duties to be carried out by the new employee(s) and pay and conditions. (1 mark)

Prepare a Person Specification outlining the 'Desired' and 'Essential' qualities looked for in the successful candidate. These might include qualifications and previous experience. (1 mark)

Publicise the vacancy. This could be done externally by advertising in papers, online, or by contacting a Recruitment Agency (Internal recruitment is when it would be advertised within an organisation, e.g. on their intranet or a staff notice board.) (1 mark)

Application forms are usually prepared by the organisation and completed by applicants. They are used by the organisation to reduce the number of candidates being called for interview. (These will often be matched to the Person Specification.) (1 mark)

The selection process most common is an interview. Here candidates will be asked a number of questions relating to the post. (Candidates might also be asked to undertake some kind of skill-test to determine their aptitude for the position.) (1 mark)

In this 'describe' question it is unlikely that marks will be given for identifying specific recruitment and selection forms e.g. Job Description. Here you are being called on to describe them. You would however always name them to show the examiner you are clear what each stage involves and then mention a couple of things that the documents contain.

8 A function of the HRM Department is to support staff training. Discuss advantages and disadvantages of staff training.

Advantages

In order to carry out a task effectively training is often necessary. For example to make the most out of a piece of machinery then staff need to be taught how to use it. (1 mark)

Staff can feel valued because employers are paying for training. This often motivates them to greater productivity. (1 mark)

Trained staff often make fewer mistakes which should save the organisation money or improve reputation. (1 mark)

Disadvantages

Training can be expensive – especially when you take into account travel and accommodation costs. It might simply not be value-for-money. (1 mark)

When the person is being trained their job either is not being done or someone else needs to do it. This can be costly and when someone else has to do the job it may create ill-feeling. (1 mark)

When a member of staff is trained it might improve their desirability and they could leave the organisation for a better job elsewhere. This results in wasted training costs and the need to recruit a new member of staff. (1 mark)

The above answers are not exhaustive, they simply illustrate the type of responses that could gain marks. If you come up with other answers ask your teacher to check that they are worth a mark.

3 The Final Examination

INTRODUCTION

It is almost impossible to guess exactly what is going to be in the final examination – so why try? Use your time to study each of the topics covered in your Higher Business Management course.

There will inevitably be some topics you find more enjoyable than others. Do not fool yourself by spending too much time on topics you find easy at the expense of the ones you find a bit difficult.

Below is a list of the topics that you will be studying during your Higher Business Management course. Next to each of the topics is a space where you can decide – approximately – how long you should spend revising each topic. A good guide is to think of how long each section of the course took to complete and base it on that. Looking at past papers can also help focus your attention on what you need to study and for how long.

As a general rule you should spend more time, minute for minute, on difficult areas than on your favourite topics. Yes really!

This does not include the practice you need to do reading as many case studies as you can so that you can practise identifying problems quickly and accurately – practise, practise, practise.

Course Content	Study/Revision Time Plan
Business in Contemporary Society	
Business Information and ICT	
Decision Making in Business	
Internal Organisation	
Marketing	
Operations	
Financial Management	
Human Resource Management	
Total	

It is important to get as much practice as you can in answering past paper questions.

WHAT DO I HAVE TO DO FOR THIS EXAMINATION?

The final examination paper is divided into two sections. Section One consists of a case study worth 50 marks and **all** the questions (usually seven or eight) in this section are **compulsory**. Section Two offers a **choice** of two questions from five extended response questions, each of which is worth 25 marks and is divided into four parts with marks ranging from 2 to 9 marks per part. A lot of writing is expected of you in this paper so it is very important that you plan your time so that you do not run out. Managing your time in the exam is very important if you are to achieve the best possible mark.

HOW MUCH TIME DO I HAVE TO COMPLETE THE PAPER?

The whole exam takes 2 hours 30 minutes – each section should therefore take no longer than 1 hour 15 minutes. But you must remember to include reading time in that calculation.

Perhaps a more realistic time should be 1 hour for Section One plus 15 minutes reading time for the case study. Similarly allocate 1 hour for Section Two – which allows 15 minutes to read **and** plan for the two questions you decide are best for you to attempt.

 Time management can make all the difference to your final mark. Make sure you remember that the whole paper involves quite a bit of reading before you start writing!

SOME GENERAL ADVICE

There is no right way to tackle the paper. You can do the sections in any order.

Some people prefer to start with Section Two where the questions tend to ask for longer, more detailed answers and where they find it easier to keep to time. Some also feel that they have crammed so much information into their heads they are just desperate to write it down and so find this easier in the more in-depth answers typical of Section Two where the questions will test you on only two or three areas of the course. Another argument for starting with Section Two is that if you are running out of time it can sometimes be easier to pick up marks quicker in Section One than in Section Two.

It must be said however, that most people start at the beginning with Section One and work their way through the paper finding the mixture of short and long answers in Section One settles them into the demands of the Higher Business Management paper. The choice is yours – just remember to keep an eye on that clock and aim to keep to your timings.

Practise past papers where you start with Section One and then move on to Section Two and then change the order with another past paper. Stick to whichever way you are happiest with – during the examination you do not have time to change your mind.

Be guided by the marks. Generally speaking a valid point merits a mark.

When deciding on which two questions to answer in Section Two put a tick beside any bits that you feel confident you know about. The questions with the most ticks are the ones you should do.

SECTION TWO *Marks*

This section should take you approximately 1 hour 15 minutes.

Answer TWO questions.

(*a*) Describe how both horizontal and vertical integration could allow an organisation to become even larger and more profitable. ✓   5

(*b*) Describe methods a limited company could use to finance a successful takeover. ✓   4

(*c*) Explain why firms use loss leaders as a pricing tactic. ✓   3

(*d*) Describe the methods available to a Public Relations department to improve the image of an organisation.   5

(*e*) Many organisations group their activities by function. ✓

Discuss other methods an organisation could use to group their activities.   8

   (25)

(*a*) Employees may undertake industrial action in an attempt to force employers to meet their demands. ✓

Describe types of industrial action that employees could take.   4

(*b*) Explain possible effects that prolonged industrial action could have on an

---

Does this seem too obvious? Sometimes candidates start to answer a question because they feel confident about ONE section and then have to start another question when they realise they can only answer that one part!

Also, remember that marks are not given for developing points (giving **additional** or **extra** examples). Just make sure when writing your answer that each point is different and not simply a repeat of a previous one.

From SQA External Assessment Report

> 'Candidates should be made aware that they are not given marks specifically for examples in addition to a point already made.'

You may like to begin your answer by

1 Defining the terms mentioned in the question, e.g.

   Describe methods a limited company could use to finance a successful takeover.

   Start of your answer:

   A limited company is owned by shareholders …

   Beginning your answer in this way may help to keep you focused on the question.

2 Keep sentences short – there is a danger when writing long sentences that you stray from the point or worse – write more than is required – losing valuable time.

3 Structure your answer in a way that reflects the number of marks allocated. Generally speaking if a question is worth three marks lay your answer out in three sentences.

   - Bullet points can sometimes be used to display answers.

   - They help you see very clearly how many points you have made and how many more you have to think of.

   - There is however a danger that when using bullet points you reduce your responses to two- or three-word answers. Don't ignore the advice given by the SQA to all candidates.

 From SQA External Assessment Report

> 'Although it is acceptable to answer in bullet format, many candidates failed to access full marks because their answers did not contain sufficient depth to address the command word.'

4   Leave a few blank lines after all your answers. If you know that you do not
    have the full number of points you can always come back to it later when you
    have had more time to think. Even when you feel you have fully answered
    a question it is still a good idea to leave space because when you proofread
    your answer at the end of the exam you might think of an additional point
    that will clarify what you have said so that the examiner is in no doubt about
    what you are trying to say.

5   If a question asks for two or three points and you can think of one more then,
    in general, you should write it down.

    This is a good idea because one of your points may not be worth a mark
    or not relevant to the question being asked. You **always** gain credit for
    any correct answers – you are not penalised for a wrong answer – no minus
    marks! However, a word of warning – be very careful here and do not let time
    run away with you. It is vital that you finish all the questions in the Higher
    Business Managment papers to ensure your best grade.

6   By drawing a simple **mindmap** it can help you when setting out a lengthy
    answer. Just put down the central theme and all the important points around
    it. For example:

Many organisations group their activities by function.

Discuss other methods an organisation could use to group their activities.

(8 marks)

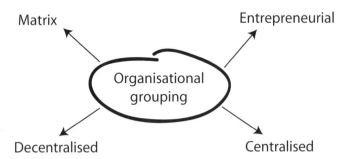

Reference to the mindmap will ensure that you do not miss out points which can
be easily forgotten when you start to flesh out earlier points.

If you want more practice in this area you can access Revision Mind Maps at
www.leckiemindmaps.com

Now down to some specifics – beginning with Section One, the case study.

SECTION ONE – CASE STUDY: LEES' OF SCOTLAND

Section One will assess not only your knowledge and understanding but also your problem solving skills and ability in decision making. This section covers all parts of the course and all questions in this section are **compulsory** – so it would be foolish to choose to only study certain areas of the course.

This section will consist of a case study of a real-life business organisation – about 750 words long, e.g. a manufacturing company such as Lees' Confectionery (2008) or a service industry such as Oban tourism (2007). Question 1 of this section always follows the same format and is there to test your ability to **apply** your understanding of management theory to the case study. In the case study, the business organisation will be or have been suffering problems or difficulties. You are required to **identify** any such problems and relate them to areas of the course.

The specific areas are:

● Marketing,
● Operations,
● Finance,
● Human Resource Management, and
● External.

You are instructed to answer using the headings specified (maximum of four areas) – you must use these headings to gain the maximum marks available. More importantly, answers to this question must relate **directly** to the case study. A common mistake is to attempt to suggest **solutions** to the problems, for which no marks are given. As well as gaining no marks, a lot of time is wasted.

 Remember, don't give solutions – no marks are awarded for solutions to the problems stated in the case study.

This question is worth 10 marks and if you practise, you can and should gain all of those marks. Think of it – 10% of your marks immediately! It is important that you practise reading this amount of information quickly and efficiently so that you can quickly **identify** the specific problems being asked for in the question.

 Remember, this question relates directly to the case study and so it often helps if you know the headings under which you have to place the problems **before** starting to read.

You may find it easier to recognise the problems if you look at the areas specified in question 1 before you start reading the case study. For best results copy down the headings – two per page is a good idea with the second heading halfway down the page. This will leave plenty of space to list the problems as you read the case study. It also allows you to add any problems you may have forgotten when you review your work at the end of the exam.

Under Marketing, your answer may be any one from the marketing mix (4Ps) – *price*, *place*, *product* and *promotion*. Sometimes being specific like this can help you focus.

As you read the case study some of the difficulties will be really easy to **identify** as parts of the material provided will be quite specific and clearly **identify** a problem. However, for others, you might have to read into the scenario presented and look more carefully to find (**identify**) the remaining problems. To gain a mark for a problem it must be put under the correct heading.

How will this question be marked?

Although there are 10 marks for this question, each section can only be awarded a maximum of 3 marks. That doesn't mean that you will get 12 marks if you manage to get three valid points under each of the four headings. But it is better to put as many problems as you can find in the case study under the relevant heading – and leave it to the examiner to decide which ones are valid and which ones will not be awarded any marks.

Also, if you are unsure between two headings then it is OK to put them under both – the examiner will credit the correct answer and ignore the one under the 'wrong' heading.

Sometimes a problem can legitimately fall under two headings – that is fine, if you really can't decide – you can put the identified problem under one or both headings – but remember you will only be awarded the mark once.

For example:

- A worldwide economic recession could be identified as a Finance problem and/or a Marketing problem and/or even an External Factor.
- Increased costs could be identified as an Operations problem and/or a Finance problem.

Take great care with this. Sometimes your own indecision (and lack of knowledge) can result in you actually losing marks. Instead of making sure you get full marks by repeating problems identified under more than one heading, you can actually end up with the minimum marks – 3 – that would be awarded if no headings were used.

 From SQA External Assessment Report

'Candidates who use no headings at all can only gain a maximum of 3 marks as do those candidates who place every problem under every heading. This should be avoided. Candidates who rewrite every problem 4 times should be made aware that not only are they wasting time, they will be awarded a maximum of 3 marks.'

The **command** word used in this Section One, Question 1 is **identify**. This means you have to be brief in your points. However, it is vital that you make sure that you are not so brief that you will not be awarded a mark.

In one recent case study problems in the Scottish skiing industry had to be identified. Someone who simply wrote the problem was a *Strong pound against the dollar* did not get a mark. The answer would have to say *Strong pound against the dollar* **means fewer American tourists are coming to ski in Scotland** as the problem is only identified in the second half of the sentence. It is always best to avoid extremely brief answers – take care with that.

From SQA External Assessment Report

'Candidates should be reminded that the answers they give in Question 1 must come from the case study. Those candidates who have knowledge of the industry or business being described do not have an advantage as marks are only given to problems included in the material.'

In the same case study about the Scottish skiing industry, many candidates identified a problem with conservationists. However in the actual case study, the problem was not with conservationists alone, but the fact that *conservationists caused the work on the proposed chairlift to be delayed*. Care must be taken that assumptions based on previous study and discussions in class with your teacher are not identified as problems within the case study you are reading during your examination.

Failure to use the headings given will result in the examiner marking the question out of a maximum of 3 marks rather than 10.

You must also remember that you are looking for the number of problems to reflect the number of marks allocated, i.e. 10. If you can come up with more problems then great! There are likely to be more than ten problems in the case study anyway – so it is better to be safe than sorry. Although the examiner will not penalise you if some of the points you write are not problems actually listed in the case study, you only get awarded marks for correct answers and you have just wasted valuable time which you may need for Section Two. Similarly, even if all the problems you identify are valid – it won't get you any extra marks.

 As you read the case study highlight or underline any sentence or phrase which you think could be a problem for management. Once you have done that you can then easily decide which area it is, e.g. Marketing or Operations.

The following pages contain two case studies (from the 2008 and 2007 examinations). To illustrate this and help you in future, problems have been highlighted.

SECTION ONE

This section should take you approximately 1 hour 15 minutes.

Read through the following information, then answer the questions which follow.

SWEET TASTE OF SUCCESS SPOILED BY SUPERMARKETS

> This paragraph contains background information

Background

Lees' main business is the manufacture of confectionery and bakery products. It can trace its roots back to 1931, when confectioner John Justice Lees allegedly botched the formula for making a chocolate fondant bar and threw coconut over it in disgust, producing the first macaroon bar. Its customers include major food retailers, food service and catering companies and other food manufacturers. It operates from 2 modern manufacturing sites in Coatbridge and Cambuslang. Lees now employs 155 staff at its Coatbridge plant, along with around 60 at the Waverley Bakery in Cambuslang, which Lees acquired for £600,000 at the beginning of 2003. Macaroon bars and snowballs have been adored by Scots for 75 years—but Lees was going nowhere until former Bell's whisky boss Raymond Miquel became Managing Director and saved the company from bankruptcy.

In recent times supermarkets have put the squeeze on Lees, but the snowball maker still plans to enter more overseas markets and expand through takeover bids. Increases in labour, transport and raw material costs cannot be passed on to consumers because of cut-throat price discounting among the major supermarket chains. Raymond Miquel said "The multiple retailers just won't accept price rises and haven't done for several years, which means we have to keep looking to new markets and new products."

The company experienced some bad times in the 1980s when sales dropped to an all time low. In 1993, the company had a balance sheet worth £350,000 and almost folded with debts of over £5 million owed to suppliers, the Clydesdale Bank and the Inland Revenue. The economic situation at the time didn't help with a worldwide recession. However, they have turned themselves around and built a new factory. Now the products are not only doing well in Scotland but are being sold in the USA, the Netherlands and Ireland. Even the King of Tonga can't get enough of them! This has resulted in a number of supermarkets and confectioners running out of stock of Lees Macaroon Bars as the company has had problems coping with increased demand.

Modernisation and transformation

Miquel saved Lees from liquidation in 1993 when he acquired the company from Northumbrian Fine Food for around £1 million. In 1993, Lees had a number of unprofitable product lines which were eventually shed by Miquel. In the 12 intervening years, however, the company has transformed itself—announcing in 2005 a rise in annual profits of 5 per cent and sales up by 9 per cent. In comparison, in 2002, the company saw sales rise but profits fall.

Miquel, by his own admission, inherited 2 run-down factories producing a handful of old-fashioned products and a very nervous workforce who were concerned for the future of their jobs. Miquel felt that many of the operations aspects of the business were in a mess. His first decision was to tackle the firm's unprofitability. Many senior managers were not performing to the standards that Miquel expected and as a result were dismissed from their posts. Next to be targeted by Miquel was the outdated 1930s style packaging. Despite working hard, the sales staff were not making enough of a profit margin for the company. This was addressed by recruiting new sales staff and training existing staff. Miquel describes his style of management as "a bit more hard nosed" than most managing directors and this has caused conflict with some of the long term managers at Lees.

The present situation

Since Miquel took control, sales of macaroon bars have surged, and Lees now sells 2.5 million every year. This represents more than 40 per cent of the company's total confectionery sales. No less popular are Lees snowballs, now selling more than 50 million a year in the UK.

Today Lees is sitting on a massive £6 million in reserve, has no debt and a large overdraft facility. It plans to expand the business overseas and to target other businesses for takeover. Miquel forecasts all kinds of possibilities to diversify, such as restaurants, upmarket tearooms and retail outlets. However, Miquel believes this will be a relatively slow process. Lees will only acquire companies which will add to their profitability, giving them further opportunities to expand in the food industry. Lees has now floated on the stock market, just over a decade after it stared liquidation in the face. It can only be a matter of time before Miquel's Lees story amazes further!

Adapted from http://thescotsman.com/business/

SECTION ONE – CASE STUDY QUESTIONS

Remember that your answer must always relate to the case study and your answer should include ONLY problems NOT solutions.

Brackets *[......]* have been used in the sample answers to show where marks would be allocated.

Total marks for a section are shown in a circle, e.g. (**3**)

Below is the question relating to this case study.

---

1   **Identify the problems faced by Lees. You should use the following headings.**

(Please identify problems only, solutions will not be credited.)

● Marketing

● Human Resource Management

● Finance

● Operations   (10 marks)

Here is an example of a weak answer to question 1 – Marketing

Marketing

— Have to look for new markets

— [Outdated 1930s-style packaging] – needs modernising   (**1**)

Why is this a weak answer?

Because it is attempting to solve the problems – *have to look for new markets,* and *needs modernising*. Only one mark will be awarded for the marketing problem of having outdated packaging.

Here is a much better answer to Marketing

Marketing

— [Cut-throat price discounting among major supermarkets]

— [Outdated 1930s-style packaging]

— [Producing only a handful of old-fashioned products]

Why is this a much better answer?

Because the points made:

✓ relate directly to the case study,

✓ are under the correct heading, and

✓ do not offer any solutions.

Although they are brief, they **identify** Marketing problems faced by the company in the case study.

Here is an example of a weak answer to question 1 – Human Resource Management

Human Resource Management

— Recruiting new sales staff is expensive

— [Inadequate sales staff in need of training]

Why is this a weak answer?

There is no mention in the case study of how expensive it is to recruit new staff. The second point is OK though because it uses the information – *senior managers not performing and sales staff not making enough of a profit margin* – to state a Human Resource Management problem. However, it could easily have achieved 2 marks if the candidate had simply stated:

● senior managers not performing well, and

● sales staff not making enough of a profit margin.

Here is an example of a better answer to question 1 – Human Resource Management

Human Resource Management

— [Many senior staff not performing well and were dismissed from their post]

— Recruiting new sales staff could cause hostility from previous workers

— [Very nervous workforce concerned for their future]

— [Conflict between new owner and some of the long-term managers]

Again the points awarded marks relate directly to the case study and are under the correct heading and do not offer any solutions. Although they are brief they identify HRM problems faced by the company in the case study.

This is an example of the benefit of trying to identify as many problems as possible. The full mark allocation has been awarded, even though one of the points identified is not a valid answer. Here are some points to note.

1   In this case the first bullet point did not need the development point – *and were dismissed from their post*. The brackets show exactly what is needed when identifying management problems.

2   In the second bullet point – *Recruiting new sales staff* – does not get any marks because it is not really mentioned in the case study as a problem for the company – *the cost of recruiting staff* or *the cost of staff training* might have been considered to be a relevant answer but this is not what is in the case study.

3   And there is nothing in the case study which mentions *hostility from previous workers*.

Here is an example of a weak answer to question 1 – Finance

Finance

— Recruiting new sales staff is expensive

— Diversification is a very slow process

Why is this a weak answer?

There is no mention of how expensive recruitment is and it could be argued that it is a problem for Human Resource Management. The second point mentioning diversification is not a problem but simply a future possibility for Lees to think about. This answer would therefore gain no marks.

Here is an example of a strong answer to Question 1 – Finance

Note again that the points awarded marks relate directly to the case study and are under the correct heading and do not offer any solutions. Although they are brief they identify **Finance** problems faced by the company in the case study.

Finance

— [Sales dropped to an all time low in 1980s]

— [Company faced bankruptcy in 1993]

— [Producing only a handful of old-fashioned products]

— [Unprofitable product lines existed]

Note that this answer contains four points – again too many as there are only 3 marks available. BUT the fourth bullet point – *unprofitable product lines existed* – could easily fit under the **Operations** heading. Better to be safe than sorry – see next heading!

Here is an example of a good response to question 1 – Operations

Note again that the points awarded relate directly to the case study and are under the correct heading and do not offer any solutions. Although they are brief they identify Operations problems faced by the company in the case study.

<u>Operations</u>

— [Increases in labour transport and raw material costs]

— [Company cannot cope with increased demand]

— [Unprofitable product lines existed]

(3)

As you can see the third point is acceptable as an Operations problem as well as a Finance problem. Therefore it is sensible to place it under both headings in case some of your earlier sections do not gain maximum marks.

There are 3 marks available for the last Operations answer shown. However, if ALL of the good example answers were from the one single answer, only 1 mark would have been available for the Operations section.

Why?

(3 for Marketing + 3 for HRM +3 for Finance +1 max for Operations) = 10.

Examiners have no problem with candidates who try and find three problems per heading – it proves to them that candidates are trying to get the full allocation of marks.

Surely it is better to be safe than sorry – you should always try and try for the maximum marks available for each section.

SECTION ONE – CASE STUDY: TOURISM IN OBAN

Let's look at another case study – this time from 2007 – Tourism in Oban.

**This section should take you approximately 1 hour 15 minutes.
Read through the following information, then answer the questions
which follow.**

OBAN HARBOURING FEARS OVER TOURISM

THE PAST

Thirty years ago the police used to stop throngs of tourists at Connel advising them that there was not a bed to be had in Oban, the famous Scottish coastal resort, just a few miles further on. Oban's stake in the tourist business was based on its harbour and the surrounding islands.

> There are no problems in this section of the case study.

There are huge hotels along the beachfront and cruise ships and yachts used to fill the bay. It became the main point of departure for many of the islands and trips to Iona and Staffa were promoted. These trips were very popular with tourists. Caledonian MacBrayne operated ferries from Oban to Mull and other islands off the West Coast of Scotland. Many large bus tour operators frequently stopped in the town.

THE PRESENT

There are now major concerns amongst local business people that the town's main asset, its waterfront, is not being properly utilised. It is claimed that despite being the natural centre for yachting in Scotland, Oban is missing out on the lucrative trade from yachters

because of a lack of vision from the local council. It is felt that not enough is being done to attract tourists from the UK and worldwide; much more promotion needs to be carried out. Oban also has a severe lack of car parking facilities and access to the North Pier is very difficult for cars and buses.

Local business leaders agree it is a disgrace that Oban's harbour has nowhere for yachters to tie up, walk ashore and spend their money. This could be worth £15 million a year to the Highlands and Islands.

OBAN YACHTS

Tony Cox, of Oban Yachts, based on Kerrera provides 56 fully serviced berths with a marine repair and maintenance service, plus a ferry to Oban. Although he is busy, he believes his business and Oban could be even busier. There are only half a dozen moorings in Oban itself. This means Oban loses out on yachters, who spend their money at nearby Dunstaffnage and Ardfern, which can take about 140 yachts each.

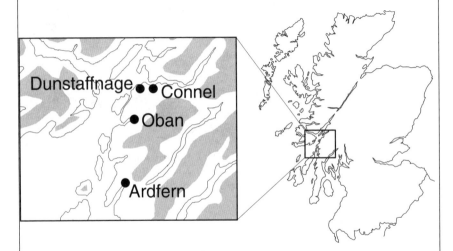

Oban Yachts brings over £300,000 into the local economy each month during the summer season. Tony Cox has invested over £750,000 into Oban Yachts over the last 3 years. However, until he sees action from the local council he is unwilling, like many other local businesses, to invest more money. Tony also has difficulties as he is never certain when busy spells can occur and has to rely on the goodwill of staff to work longer hours at short notice.

EEUSK RESTAURANT

Alan MacLeod, who runs The Eeusk Restaurant on the North Pier, is also concerned for the future of tourism in Oban. He feels that there need to be more attractions to entertain the tourists. Alan insists this would help reduce unemployment in the area, however, there is a lack of experienced workers in Oban. Few people want to work in the tourist industry as it mainly provides seasonal work. Staff are given short-term contracts which make the jobs in restaurants and hotels less appealing. Most of the staff in Alan's restaurant are students or part-time workers resulting in a high staff turnover. Alan frequently needs to provide training for the new employees which can be costly.

LOCAL COUNCIL

The local council is taking steps to improve the facilities in Oban. The North Pier is to be developed to include new toilet and showering facilities, with tourists in mind. New restaurants are also planned for the North Pier. The local council is carrying out consultation with stakeholders in an attempt to highlight problems which may have been overlooked.

OTHER ISSUES

One factor that the local council cannot overcome is the weather. The West of Scotland is notorious for rainy, wet summers. This does not appeal to tourists and many people prefer to holiday in a warmer climate. This is a proven stumbling block as with any spell of hot weather the number of visitors to Oban increases. During the warm spell in July and August 2005, the Tourist Information Centre reported that record numbers were visiting the Centre, over 6,200 in one day alone. Many of these tourists were trying to find somewhere to stay and Oban was back to the good times, with not a bed to be found in any hotel or bed and breakfast establishment!

With the drop in tourism over the past few years, linked specially to the lack of American visitors, due to the rise in terrorism in Europe, it is difficult for local businesses to survive. Hopefully, Oban can again become the place to visit during the summer months. The local business community would certainly flourish as attractions, such as McCaig's Folly, Gylen Castle on Kerrera and the Argyllshire Gathering are second to none.

Adapted from an article in The Herald, 28 August 2005, by David Ross

SECTION ONE – CASE STUDY QUESTIONS

1   Identify the problems of the tourist industry in Oban. You should use the following headings. (Please identify problems only, solutions will not be credited.)

● Marketing

● Finance

● Human Resources

● External Factors   (10 marks)

 From SQA External Assessment Report

'This year it was possible for problems to fall under one or more of the headings, e.g. "lack of car parking facilities" was credited either under the Marketing heading or the External heading. Candidates must be careful not to repeat points as they are wasting time and gaining no further marks.'

When the case study refers to a service industry rather than a business producing goods, try and remember that the marketing mix (4Ps) – price, place, product and promotion – are still important in helping you to identify problems.

Here is an example of a weak answer to question 1 – Marketing

Marketing

The image of the service is not high enough re brand image. It does not appeal to customers and so it is hard to achieve brand loyalty. Customers might go to competitors and the industry loses its customers and may mean that they will have to spend more money to attract these customers. The industry does not seem to carry out market research to get to know its customers. They should build more car parks.   (0)

Why is this answer weak?

Because it is attempting to solve the problems.

Also it is a rambling answer which does not reflect the command word **identify**. However, the main problem with this answer is that it **does not refer to the case study,** but appears to contain the assumptions of the candidate – perhaps based on class work and discussion.

Be very careful that you read the case study to identify the problems within it. Don't try and guess what the problems are or try to solve them. This is perhaps the ONLY question where being brief and to the point is the best way to achieve the maximum marks available.

Here is a much better answer.

 Marketing

— [Not enough is being done to attract tourists from UK and worldwide]

— [Lack of moorings for yachters to tie up and walk ashore]

— [Lack of car parking facilities]   (3)

Why is this a better answer?

This candidate has remembered the features of the marketing mix. The first point is the most obvious Marketing issue facing the Oban tourist industry (promotion). The second and third points would fall into the product category. Although they are brief they identify Marketing problems faced by the tourist industry outlined in the case study.

Also, as previously stated, the points made:

✓ relate directly to the case study, and

✓ are under the correct heading, and

✓ do not offer any solutions.

This particular case study has more marketing problems as follows.

- Main asset, the town's waterfront is not being used properly

- Not enough attractions to entertain tourists

- Lack of accommodation during busy spells – this could also be an external problem

- Competition from nearby towns – again this could also be seen as an external problem

Remember though – you can't get 2 marks for the same point under different headings.

Here is an example of a weak answer to question 1 – Finance

Finance

— They are not making a possible £15 million a year

— [Local businessmen unwilling to invest more money]

— It appears that the industry is not preparing budgets – so running out of money

Why is this a weak answer?

The only relevant point (based on the information in the case study) is that local businessmen are unwilling to invest anymore (*until … action from the local council*). The other two points again show that although they both make reference to finance, they are assumptions made rather than problems being **identified**.

Here is an example of a strong answer to question 1 – Finance

Finance

— [Lack of sufficient investment from the local council]

— [Provision of training for new employees can be costly]

— [Income from tourism is seasonal]

Note again that the marks awarded relate directly to the case study and do not offer any solutions. Although they are brief they identify **Finance** problems faced by the tourist industry in Oban.

Here is an example of a weak answer to question 1 – Human Resources

Human Resources

— High unemployment in the area

— Staff are only given short-term contracts

— [Fewer people want to work in the industry]

Why is this a weak answer?

The fact that there is high unemployment is the area is not a problem – it is the *lack of experienced workers in Oban* that is the problem. Similarly the fact that staff are given short-term contracts is not the problem in itself but that *it makes the work less appealing*. The third point states that and is therefore awarded a mark.

Here is an example of a strong answer to question 1 – Human Resources

Human Resources Management

— [Lack of experienced workforce in the tourist industry]

— [High staff turnover in industry makes recruitment and training costly]

— [In busy spells, have to rely on goodwill of staff to work at short notice]

The last part of this question requires the identification of **External Factors** that are problems for the industry. Sometimes a common mistake made by candidates is to list everything under this heading. Remember this is not a good idea and can actually lose marks. However, this section can ensure that full marks are gained – if care is taken not to be too repetitive.

Here is an example of a good answer to question 1 – External Factors

External Factors

— [Rainy wet summers do not appeal to tourists]

— Many people prefer to holiday in a warmer climate

— [Nearby towns are more appealing because of better facilities]

— [American tourists are put off travel because of the rise in terrorism]

The R shows that no marks are gained for saying the same thing twice.

Now you have 10% of your marks sorted – what next?

SECTION ONE – QUESTIONS 2-7/8

Compulsory – you have no choice

The remaining questions in Section One are made up of a variety of short questions (usually 1 or 2 marks) and extended response questions (anything between 3-6 marks, depending on the area covered and the command word used). There tend to be between six and seven more questions in total making up the remaining 40 marks (exactly half the examination paper – 50% in total).

As already pointed out, these questions are compulsory and aim to test your knowledge of every area of the course. **You therefore cannot afford to miss out any area of the course in your revision programme.** Although many of these questions refer to the case study (stimulus material) you are unlikely to find any answers to the questions in the actual passages. Questions in this section will make a general reference to the business in the case study but do not limit you to that business only.

 From SQA External Assessment Report

'Reference to stimulus material is only essential in Section One, Question 1. However if valid points which incorporate the stimulus material are made in the remaining questions, candidates will be credited with the marks.'

The main thing to remember is that any point you make must be RELEVANT (valid) to the question being asked – and if that means incorporating something from the case study that is just fine.

For example:

> ## The ... restaurant has a problem with high staff turnover. This requires frequent induction training.
>
> i. Describe the term induction training. (1 mark)
> ii. Outline the benefits of induction training. (4 marks)

An answer to the above would not need to mention or refer specifically to a restaurant but if it helped to use a restaurant while outlining the benefits that would be fine.

The following sample answer makes reference to a restaurant.

i. Induction training is training [given to new employees when they first start working in a business like a restaurant so that they know how the business works]. 1 mark

ii. The benefits of induction training are:

- [Health and Safety issues with regard to food preparation can be pointed out to new staff.]   1 mark

- [New staff are integrated more quickly into the restaurant team.]   1 mark

- [New staff are aware of the layout of the restaurant and where things are kept.]   1 mark

- [Staff are more motivated if they feel welcome.]   1 mark

Why is this a good answer?

Because it shows that the writer understands the concept of staff training, its benefits and how it applies to a specific business. Also the use of bullet points in part (ii) is acceptable as the question uses the command word **outline**. It also helps ensure that a 4-mark question has four clear points being outlined.

Occasionally a question may be phrased in such a way that you have to take account of the type of business in the case study.

For example:

> **Describe and justify an appropriate training method for a manufacturing company such as Harris Tweed.**
>
> (4 marks)

In this case any acceptable answer **must focus on a manufacturing company** and not just any type of business. You have to make sure you read the question fully and understand what is being asked.

Here are some more Section One examples of poor answers and much better ones – so that you can recognise and hopefully practise the type of answer you need to provide to gain the maximum marks available for each question you attempt.

> **Describe a pricing tactic which could be used to ensure a new product or service appears exclusive.**
>
> (2 marks)

Note this question uses the command word **describe** but the mark allocation is 2 marks (the previous one was for 1 mark). You have to make sure you write with enough detail to gain those marks. Remember that the question is only looking for a description of ONE pricing tactic *which could be used to ensure a new product or service appears exclusive.*

The following sample answer is just a repeat of the question with two pricing tactics simply **identified** or **named**. Rewriting the question is a technique often used to settle into an answer but care should be taken when doing this. It is easy to think that this makes a 'one word answer' acceptable. It does not – it is just takes up valuable time and gains no marks.

A pricing tactic which could be used to ensure a new product or service appears exclusive is market skimming. Another method is premium pricing.

This example gains **no marks at all** as is does not **describe** anything – but merely **names/identifies** – and no marks are made 'available' just because more than one pricing tactic is named/identified.

This answer also shows that the question has not been fully read – ***Describe*** a *pricing tactic* so any answer should refer to **one** pricing tactic. Also, no account has been made of the second part of the question – *used to ensure a new product or service appears exclusive.*

See below for better answers.

[Market skimming is a method of pricing often used where a product is highly priced when entering the market for the first time.] (1 mark) (It consists of setting an initially high price for the product.) [The price can then be lowered to target another segment of the market.] (1 mark)

Or

[Premium pricing is a method of pricing adopted by businesses offering high-quality premium goods or services where image is important.] (1 mark) (Also called prestige pricing), this strategy helps to [attract status-conscious consumers who believe the high price signals that they are a member of an exclusive group.] (1 mark)

Both of these answers understand the question – which requires the answer to take into account *to ensure … appears exclusive*. The bracketed parts **( )** of the examples are not really required to achieve the mark – the marks could be awarded without them. However, it does help to make the answer much more rounded and sophisticated. In turn, the examiner who is marking your work will be confident that you have a very good knowledge of the topic in question.

Read the question properly before answering.

In many cases, the reason for poor performance in this section in particular is that many candidates fail to read the question properly. As mentioned above the first example proved that the candidate simply read 'pricing tactic' and did not read the rest of the question.

> ## Describe the advantages to an organisation of having a website. (6 marks)

On first reading, this question seems to be quite easy and most candidates would feel they know a lot about the internet and websites – enough certainly to get 6 marks.

Look at the first response.

Advantages of a website are:

- cheap to run,
- global market,
- available 24/7,
- can be accessed from home,
- cheaper than buying from shops, and
- colourful with images and fonts etc.

This response would gain no marks at all.

Why?

I am sure you now realise that the above answer is a list – there are no descriptions at all on any of the bullet points. As well as the brevity of the 'list' the question also specified *advantages to an organisation* and some of the points 'listed' could be seen as relating to the customer's point of view. So it is a poor answer on two counts.

Remember the command word **describe**, commands a **description** – not naming or identifying.

Have a look at the second response.

The advantages of having a website to an organisation include that they are relatively inexpensive to obtain. The [website is available to people all over the world]. This means that [anyone with access to the internet could stumble across a website which makes it a valuable marketing asset]. [The organisation allows customers to buy products/services online using e-commerce]. E-commerce has several advantages. The company [saves money on buying premises and employing staff as they would have to do when operating a store]. People can buy products from the comfort of their home even if they are in a different country from where the organisation is based. The firm [can use the website to promote the product or service that they offer]. This is nowhere near as expensive as TV advertising. The website can be regularly updated by someone who is in charge of the website. The website can be made more attractive by the use of videos, images, colour, text etc. [It can also be made interactive to attract people back to the website.]

(6)

The main fault with this response is that, although it would probably get the 6 marks available, it is very wordy and goes into too much detail for the command word **describe**. Another fault with this answer is that it is quite repetitive and goes off the point.

This answer is a good example of:

🖑 when NOT to use examples (made attractive by text etc.), and

🖑 that development points (This is nowhere near as expensive as TV advertising) do not gain any extra marks and in fact can result in the loss of valuable time for other parts of the question.

Care should be taken to write enough detail to get the marks allocated but not to such an extent that you run out of time. This may seem confusing, but plenty of practice doing past papers will make it easier. In the above example the square brackets show where marks could have been allocated by an examiner.

A much better response, which would have taken less time and be less confusing for the examiner to read and mark, could be as follows.

The advantages of having a website to an organisation include that the [website is available to people all over the world]. This [makes it a valuable marketing asset by linking to other websites]. [The organisation can allow customers to buy products/services online using e-commerce]. [This saves money on buying premises and employing staff as they would have to do when operating a store]. The firm [can use the website to promote the product or service that they offer]. [It can also be made interactive to attract people back to the website through email.] **(6)**

It is basically the same answer but the long and rambling sentences have been cut and each sentence is to the point and answers the question – **describe** *the* **advantages** *to an* **organisation** *of having a* **website** – in an efficient manner. Also note that there is no use of bullet points in this answer.

Bullet points are OK when answering questions which contain the command words **identify** or **outline** – but are best avoided for other command words.

All of the examples in this section so far have illustrated the use of the command words **outline** and **describe**. **Section One** of the exam paper will have approximately five or six parts of the questions using the **describe** command word. In other words, testing your knowledge of your study of Business Management.

The remaining parts will feature more demanding command words – **explain, discuss** or **compare/distinguish.**

Explain

There are some questions which, at first glance, look 'easy'. This type of question invariably involves the use of the command word **explain** added to what appears on first reading to be a very well-known part of the course – probably something previously studied at Standard Grade and/or Intermediate level.

> Lees changed the packaging of their products which made them more eye-catching and appealing to consumers. Explain five other methods of extending a product's life cycle. (5 marks)

Two warnings:

1 the stem already contains an example of a method of extending a product's life cycle, and

2 the command word **explain** means that the answer needs a bit more than simply stating the methods of extending the life cycle.

 From SQA External Assessment Report

'This question looked very easy on the surface. However the use of the command word "explain" made the question appropriate for a Higher level paper.'

A weak response – gaining no marks at all – would be:

- improving the product,
- changing the price of the product,
- extending the product line,
- changing the promotion methods, and
- changing the way the product is packaged.

All of the above methods would extend the life cycle of a product.

Why is this a weak answer?

Firstly it is a list of methods and secondly it contains a method already mentioned in the stem. To gain marks for this type of question, a candidate would have to use examples to successfully **explain** a point they have made.

A good answer therefore would be as follows.

[Improving the product by <u>adding additional features, e.g. new and improved ingredients</u>] would extend the life cycle of a product. When a [market group has <u>reached saturation point</u>, the price could be lowered so that more people could afford it and want to buy it.] A [change in the method of advertising, e.g. <u>celebrity endorsement</u>, may give the product extra publicity and so increase sales.] [Changing the channel of distribution by <u>selling the product using the internet</u> may get new customers previously unable to be reached.] Finally [changing the name of the product, <u>e.g. *Opal Fruits* to *Starburst*</u>, may reach new customers.]

(5)

The brackets show exactly where the marks could be allocated and the underlined words are necessary to gain the marks available for an **explain** question.

You must try and recognise when you need to illustrate your knowledge and give an example to get just 1 mark. The best example of when this is necessary is if the question asks to **explain** a method as illustrated in the previous example.

The next example requires a detailed description – to prove not only your knowledge but your understanding of the term in question.

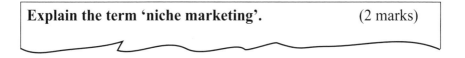
Explain the term 'niche marketing'.   (2 marks)

A good answer would have to be more than a simple definition or description. It would have to be detailed enough to ensure that there was no confusion with similar marketing terms. Questions using the command word **explain**, must be detailed enough to make sure the examiner knows that you have knowledge AND understanding – in this particular case, of the term *niche marketing*.

Niche marketing is where a [business aims a product at a particular, often very small, segment of the market where customers' needs and wants are clearly identified]. This type of marketing [helps to overcome the competition in the short-term as other businesses are not aware of it.]

(2)

The reason this is such a good answer is that it goes a bit further than a simple description as shown by where the marks are awarded by use of the square brackets. Again the use of bullet points would be inappropriate for this type of question – so don't be tempted to use them as there is a danger that your answer will be too brief.

 Sometimes it is necessary to provide two points when a question uses the command word 'explain'.

There are other types of questions that use the command word **explain** which do not always need examples to illustrate your knowledge. These types of questions usually ask you to **explain** the **benefits** of a course of action. Other questions ask you to **explain why** management take a course of action. In this case you need to try and use words like *because, as this would result in, etc.*

Example 1 – Explain benefits

Many organisations choose to delayer. Explain the benefits of delayering to an organisation.   (3 marks)

 From SQA External Assessment Report

'It is important to note the word "benefits" in this question. Some candidates merely gave a description of Delayering, accompanied in some cases by diagrams. Therefore they were not answering the actual question being asked and were not credited with the marks.'

The following response is not very good for several reasons – can you spot them?

The benefits of Delayering are:

— [since there are not as many managers the payroll is reduced]

— decision making is quicker

— communication is quicker

Why is this a weak response?

The command word is **explain** – and this answer uses a stem and bullet points. This style of answer is not to be recommended. Firstly, it encourages the use of lists rather than proper explanation. Remember the question is looking for a description. The one mark allocated to this example is not the description of Delayering – *there are not as many managers* – but the completion of the description which explains the benefit from that particular feature of Delayering – *payroll is reduced*.

The other two 'benefits' listed are not acceptable IN ANY TYPE of answer. When using statements like *decision making is quicker/cheaper,* always finish by using 'than e.g. ...'.

A much better answer – achieving the full mark allocation could be as follows.

 Delayering is the removal of layers of management thereby 'flattening' the organisation. [As this results in fewer managers, the organisation may save money on salaries]. This can also [help to improve productivity as the delegation of responsibility can be motivating to workers.] Moreover, a company is [likely to be more responsive to changes in the market because decision making takes less time than before.] ③

Why is this a good answer?

Not only does it begin by briefly describing the term 'Delayering' it flows very well. It illustrates not only the knowledge of the candidate but also an understanding of the effects of this type of restructuring decision by an organisation.

Example 2 – Explain why

> ## Explain why firms can have a healthy profit but experience cash flow problems.   (4 marks)

The following response is not very good for several reasons.

Firms can have a healthy profit but experience cash flow problems if:

— [they are allowing customers too long a credit period, reducing the amount of cash available]

— they are not keeping a tight control of expenses

— they have too many outstanding debtors

Why is this not a good response?

The command word is **explain** – and this answer uses a stem and bullet points – not to be recommended. The 1 mark allocated to this example is because it fully **explains** how the time taken for customers to pay can cause lack of immediate cash. The second 'reason' listed is not even correct – in fact it shows a total lack of understanding of profit and cash flow. The third point is merely a repeat of the first point – so no extra marks awarded.

A much better answer – achieving the full mark allocation could be as follows.

A firm can have [too much money tied up in stock which reduces the amount of cash available for immediate use]. [A firm's debtors may not be repaying on time which can worsen a firm's cash position.] Moreover, a firm may [have large loans for which the repayments are very costly because of high interest rates.] Finally, a firm may [have had to invest in new and expensive equipment which could reduce the amount of cash circulating in the business.]

> When answering questions asking to explain benefits or explain why, it is a good idea to use words or phrases like – *because, which, as this results in, etc* as these words remind you to Complete the answer fully.

There are other types of questions which use the command word **explain** which require the answer to incorporate **advantages** and **disadvantages** of a management decision or course of action.

> Organisations often use an entrepreneurial structure. Explain the advantages and disadvantages of an entrepreneurial structure to an organisation. (4 marks)

 From SQA External Assessment Report

'In order to gain marks in this question, it is essential to explain why a feature of an entrepreneurial structure is an advantage to an organisation ... Some answers did not contain enough detail to be given the mark ...'

- A good way to tackle this type of question is to **identify** a feature (e.g. few decision makers) and then **explain** how it is an **advantage** (e.g. can be beneficial because it allows major decisions to be made quickly) or a **disadvantage** (e.g. however workers may feel less motivated as they are not involved in the decision making process). In this way you will be able to present a more balanced answer which again illustrates not only knowledge but understanding of Internal Organisational Structures. It also helps you to resist the temptation to list the **advantages** and **disadvantages** using bullet points.

- It is also wise to try and give equal weight to both **advantages** and **disadvantages** – check the mark allocation. If the question is worth 4 marks, it makes sense to try and give two advantages and two disadvantages.

An acceptable answer would be as follows.

 An entrepreneurial structure is one where there are only one or two key decision makers. This can be [an advantage when decisions have to be made quickly on a daily basis.] (1 mark) There is also a [greater chance that decisions are accurate as the key decision makers usually have the most expertise.] (1 mark) However disadvantages could be that [the lack of consultation with other staff may be demotivating for them] (1 mark) and also [stress levels can be very high for the one or two staff responsible for making the decisions.] (1 mark)

 When answering questions which ask for advantages and disadvantages it is a good idea to try and give equal importance to each.

Take care with this – try not to 'list' advantages and disadvantages, even if they are full sentences. Using lists is a good way to study and remember points easily. Many solutions in books and on the SQA website use 'lists' as bullet points under headings (e.g. <u>Advantages</u> and <u>Disadvantages</u>) – but these are merely guidelines outlining the points that need to be covered. However, remember listing descriptions is OK when the command word is **describe** the advantages or disadvantages but NOT when explaining them.

The following example shows that the candidate has indeed remembered the **advantages** and **disadvantages** of an entrepreneurial structure but has failed to **explain** why they are advantages and disadvantages to the organisation. It would not be awarded any marks.

 An entrepreneurial structure is when the organisation is led by one person. The advantages and disadvantages of an entrepreneurial structure are:

<u>Advantages</u>:

- Decisions are made by few managers
- Decisions are made quickly

<u>Disadvantages</u>

- Top managers have heavy workloads
- Staff are demotivated

Discuss

Another command word which needs careful attention to detail is **discuss**. This command word can be used simply as a statement or with the addition of the **advantages** and **disadvantages** of a particular situation.

 When beginning a **discuss** question it is a good idea to start with a simple **outline** or description to set the scene.

Example 1 – Discuss a management function

Discuss the role of appraisal and its ability to motivate staff.

(6 marks)

The following is a weak answer to this type of question.

 Appraisal can motivate staff on many levels. Staff will feel as if they are needed. Appraisal could mean promotion or a pay rise. If staff feel they are needed they will be self-motivated. Staff will be more determined to get on and work hard.

(0)

Why is this a weak answer?

This answer does not show that the writer understands what the **role** of appraisal is therefore has not been able to comment (**discuss**) how appraisal can motivate staff.

The following answer is a strong answer and gains the full mark allocation

 An appraisal is a meeting between a manager and an employee. It often occurs once a year and they [usually discuss the employee's performance over a given time.] (1 mark) These meetings [help to motivate staff as they are given feedback on their performance] (1 mark) and are [set targets on how to improve.] (1 mark) Employers [may decide on the future training requirements that the employee may need] (1 mark) and this can [increase staff motivation if they know that they will be trained and develop new skills.] (1 mark) However, an appraisal is [only beneficial if there is a good relationship between employer and employee so that positive and negative aspects can be discussed without resentment.] (1 mark)

(6)

This is a good example of how to make sure full marks are gained for this type of question. Note that there are no bullet points and the answer flows in a fairly logical manner. Although not always necessary, it is better to give a balanced answer which not only discusses the positive aspects of the topic concerned – *help to motivate staff as they are given feedback on their performance*, but also rounds off with a final statement pulling the answer together – *only beneficial if there is a good relationship between employer and employee so that positive and negative aspects can be discussed without resentment.*

The command word **discuss** is best answered using:

- an introduction of some sort (can be an outline or description), followed by
- the required amount of points (see mark allocation),
- a sentence or paragraph pulling all the points together (refer to the question and introduction) to bring the 'discussion' to a close.

Example 2 – Discuss with advantages and disadvantages

Wholesalers buy goods in large quantities directly from manufacturers.

Discuss the advantages and disadvantages to a manufacturer of using a wholesaler. (5 marks)

Warning!

A common mistake when answering this type of question is to misread it and **list** or **outline** the advantages and disadvantages and to do so from the point of view of the wholesaler.

 From SQA External Assessment Report

'Many candidates failed to understand the roles of wholesalers and manufacturers.'

The following is an example of a good answer, gaining maximum points.

 The wholesaler provides the link between the manufacturer and the retailer. Advantages of a manufacturer using a wholesaler [is that time can be saved trying to get their products to individual retailers – a saving of time and money spent on transport costs.] (1 mark) [As wholesalers buy goods in bulk, this would also save the manufacturer being left with unsold obsolete stock.] (1 mark) This means [valuable capital is not tied up in unsold stock.] (1 mark) However, manufacturers [may feel that they have less control over how the product is presented to customers] (1 mark) and may also [experience a reduction in overall profits because of using a 'middleman'.] (1 mark)

(5)

Why is this a good answer?

The answer to this question takes full account of the marks available and although it is for 5 marks – so equal marks for **advantages** and **disadvantages** are not possible – the answer is balanced and flowing. The use of the introductory sentence illustrates an understanding of the link between the manufacturer and wholesaler. The absence of bullet points means that there is no temptation to list the **advantages** and **disadvantages**, as shown in previous examples.

Two command words and a stem

Questions often start with a 'stem' which is a general statement designed to focus your attention. Care must be taken when reading the stem of a question so that your answer shows that you have read and understood it.

> Government aid helped finance new developments.
> Describe and justify two other sources of long term finance which could be chosen by firms undertaking such large scale developments. (4 marks)

The important thing about this question is that the stem states that government aid helped to finance something AND it uses two command words.

Here is an example of a weak answer and a common mistake made by candidates.

A firm could look to venture capitalists for a source of long-term finance. A firm could also apply for a grant which would mean that they would not have to pay it off.

(0)

This answer would not get any marks.

Why not?

Because there is no attempt made to **describe** – simply **naming** venture capitalists as a source of long-term finance is not enough. Also, *government aid* is mentioned in the question therefore sources of finance obtained from government in the form of grants cannot be given any credit. Finally, no attempt has been made to **justify** (i.e. give reasons for) your choice of sources of long-term finance.

A much better answer is shown below.

The firm could [approach venture capitalists who offer finance in return for part ownership of the firm in return.] (1 mark for the description) The main reason a firm would choose this route is [because these lenders are willing to take more risks than banks.] (1 mark for the justification/ reason) The firm could also [issue shares in the company allowing investors to buy a share in the company.] (1 mark for the description) This would [raise very large sums of money without incurring interest.] (1 mark for the justification/reason)

(4)

When looking at solutions to past papers realise that the published answers are often condensed to save space. Do not rely on the brevity of many published answers to score top marks. They are only a guide or summary of acceptable answers.

SECTION TWO – EXTENDED RESPONSE QUESTIONS

This section of the examination paper will contain five questions from which you have to complete two. This gives you the opportunity to choose the questions which will enable you to gain the most marks. It is therefore important that you take some time out from answering questions to deciding which of the two questions will give you the best opportunity to maximise your grade. As previously shown, some people like to use ticks beside the parts of each question they feel they can answer easily, a cross beside the ones they don't feel they could answer in enough detail and maybe a question mark beside one they feel they could answer a bit (maybe not enough for the mark allocation). It will then be obvious which questions suit your strengths.

If you fail to plan you plan to fail!

	SECTION TWO	*Marks*
	This section should take you approximately 1 hour 15 minutes.	
	Answer TWO questions.	

(*a*) Describe how both horizontal and vertical integration could allow an organisation to become even larger and more profitable. ✓ — **5**

(*b*) Describe methods a limited company could use to finance a successful takeover. ✓ — **4**

(*c*) Explain why firms use loss leaders as a pricing tactic. ✓ — **3**

(*d*) Describe the methods available to a Public Relations department to improve the image of an organisation. — **5**

(*e*) Many organisations group their activities by function. ✓
Discuss other methods an organisation could use to group their activities. — **8**

(25)

(*a*) Employees may undertake industrial action in an attempt to force employers to meet their demands. ✓
Describe types of industrial action that employees could take. — **4**

(*b*) Explain possible effects that prolonged industrial action could have on an

The questions in this section are integrated which means that they will cover two or three areas of the syllabus. They will also each use a mixture of command words like **outline** and **describe** and **explain** and more challenging command words like **distinguish/compare, discuss**. Each of the questions is designed to ensure that one should not be easier or more difficult than another – assuming you have studied and understood the whole course.

Remember – you have a choice.

Look over each of the questions and grade them according to which ones you are able to fully answer. It is likely that one or more bits of a question will give you some difficulty. You must weigh up the questions and see which ones will maximise your overall score.

The examiner will mark questions in the order that you write them into your answer book. If you start a question and then decide early on to abandon it to do another question make sure you score it out or this will be the question that will be marked by the examiner.

Build into your routine time to proofread your work. Ensure that what you wanted to say is actually what you have said. Remember, the examiner does not know what you are *trying* to say.

All of the advice for writing good answers given in Section One is exactly the same as for Section Two. The main difference between the two sections is the element of choice – there are bound to be units that you are better at than others.

General Advice

Questions may well start with a 'stem' which is a general statement designed to focus your attention. The questions will then be divided into four or five sub parts such as (a), (b), (c) etc. Each of these parts are generally unrelated to the previous part of the question. Where a question is divided into (i), (ii) etc then this is an indication that the parts are related and so you should take account what you have written in answer to (i) before tackling (ii). Equally, check what (ii) is asking so that you do not end up answering it in (i).

For example:

<blockquote>

(a) Organisations continually try to obtain primary information about the market in which they operate. Describe the advantages and disadvantages of three types of field research an organisation could use to obtain primary information.   (8 marks)

(b) Explain the various means of sampling that could be used to obtain a cross section of views when carrying out market research.   (4 marks)

(c) (i) Discuss the ways in which divestment and demerger can assist the growth of an organisation.   (4 marks)

    (ii) Describe other methods of growth.   (5 marks)

(d) Describe how organisations such as the Prince's Trust, banks and Local Enterprise Agencies could provide assistance to a new business.   (4 marks)

    (25 marks)

</blockquote>

Take time to read each question. A common mistake is to jump into answering part (a) and (b) only to discover that you do not have a clue how to answer (c) or (d). This will cost you valuable time in the exam – time you do not have.

Looking at the question above – parts (a) and (b) may be tempting because it is an area you have studied and feel confident about (with a total of 12 marks – less than half). However the remaining 13 marks – parts (c) and (d) – may be from a part of the course that you are less confident about. The choice of questions is yours but make the choice which gives you the maximum opportunity to excel.

Final command words

There are two more command words that have not been illustrated so far. These are

• compare

and

• distinguish.

Sometimes candidates have problems gaining full marks for these questions – not because they do not know the answers to the question posed but because they do not really understand that to achieve the maximum marks complete comparisons or complete distinctions have to be made. In other words, to gain 3 marks, three separate comparisons or distinctions need to be made. The only difference between **compare** and **distinguish** is that **compare** allows you to state similarities **as well as** differences whereas **distinguish** only needs differences.

Distinguish

> **Distinguish between delayering and downsizing.**
>
> (3 marks)

 From SQA External Assessment Report

'Many candidates failed to understand the difference between delayering and downsizing. The command word used in this question was "distinguish" and therefore the difference between delayering and downsizing had to be made clearly in order to gain the marks.'

The example below illustrates an answer which gives three separate points but only gains 1 mark. Remember that two separate, distinguishing points need to be made to gain 1 mark.

 [Delayering is when an organisation cuts down on their levels, usually management levels, in order to become more efficient. Downsizing is when an organisation cuts down on unnecessary staff in the organisation.] This allows the company to save money. **(1)**

There are no half marks awarded so even though there appears to be a point made with no mark awarded, it is incomplete.

Here is a good example of this type of answer.

 [Delayering is the removal of layers of management to flatten the organis-ation structure. On the other hand downsizing is actually changing the size and focus of a business to a smaller scale.] (1 mark) [Delayering saves the cost of management wages whereas downsizing saves costs on the wages on all levels of workers.] (1 mark) [Delayering does not always mean that production output is reduced however downsizing usually results in removing excess capacity within the organisation.] (1 mark) **(3)**

Note that two distinct points need to be made to gain one mark. The use of words or phrases like *on the other hand, whereas, however, as opposed to*, can help you to link any points you make.

Compare

Compare the objectives of a plc to those of a public sector organisation. (3 marks)

 From SQA External Assessment Report

'The question asked candidates to compare the objectives of a plc with a public sector organisation. Only very good candidates received full marks here as the instruction to compare was ignored and only a list of objectives given.'

 [One of the main objectives of both a public sector organisation and a plc is to maximise profits – although sometimes public sector organisations may just be required to operate within a budget with no profit making.] (1 mark) [One of the main objectives of a plc is to increase market share, whereas a public sector organisation's main objective is to provide a service.] (1 mark) [Both organisations have the objective of improving their social responsibility, which is sometimes outlined in their mission statement.] (1 mark) ③

Note that, as with the command word **distinguish**, two distinct points need to be made to gain 1 mark. The use of words or phrases like *on the other hand, whereas, however, as opposed to*, when illustrating differences can help you to link any points you make. The use of the word *both* can also help illustrate similarities.

When attempting the Extended Response Questions in Section Two you must always apply the command words appropriately.

A final word from the SQA External Assessment Report

 From SQA External Assessment Report

'Those candidates who are able to handle the command words, tend to perform better as they are able to answer what is being asked in the question and do not simply write down everything they know about a topic.'
AND
'Candidates should be encouraged to read questions very carefully and actually answer what is being asked.'

If you follow these suggestions – you should boost your grade in Higher Business Management.

Conclusion

Preparing for any examination can be both stressful and physically exhausting. No one said it would be easy. But realise that sitting an examination is also an opportunity for you to shine and show how much you understand about a particular subject. A lot has got to do with being positive about life-experiences and trying to take control of a situation rather than being a victim. Confidence often comes from being prepared. Use your time wisely when studying for all your exams. Plan how much time you are going to devote to each unit or section. Build into your study time 'contingency plans' – extra time in case something comes up that prevents you from sticking to your original study schedule.

Examination time can be very stressful and it is easy to fall out with brothers, sisters, mum, dad, friends, teachers… It is probably true that no one does understand what you are going through but don't let that make you want to give up. There are times when we all have to play the prima donna – slam doors, state we will never speak to so-and-so ever again, sulk and even row. Realise that you might not be the easiest person in the world to live with at this time so give everyone, including yourself, a break.

In the weeks building up to your final exam eat sensibly, not too much garbage, and get plenty of sleep – leave remote controls, iplayers, mobiles in the kitchen when you go to bed. Avoid time-stealers like deciding to tidy your room the night before your Higher Business Management exam! Avoid social network sites when you should be studying. Also realise that at your age it is unlikely that you really do need to check text messages every 5 minutes – nothing your friends say is likely to be that urgent.

The study of Business Management is a valuable subject not only to get into university or employment but also because it is about the world we live in. At various points in your life you will look back on your study of Business Management and realise with a degree of satisfaction 'I know why they do that…'

It is usual for study books to end with the phrase 'good luck'. I prefer to think that luck is something you create for yourself. Study hard, prepare well and you will have luck in your Business Management exam.